I0826630

RICHARD FOREMAN

PLAYS WITH FILMS

Selected Other Works by
Richard Foreman

The Manifestos & Essays

Bad Boy Nietzsche! & Other Plays

Paradise Hotel & Other Plays

My Head Was a Sledgehammer: Six Plays

No-Body: A Novel in Parts

Unbalancing Acts: Foundations for a Theater

Love & Science: Selected Music-Theatre Texts

RICHARD FOREMAN

PLAYS WITH FILMS

Edited by Rainer J. Hanshe

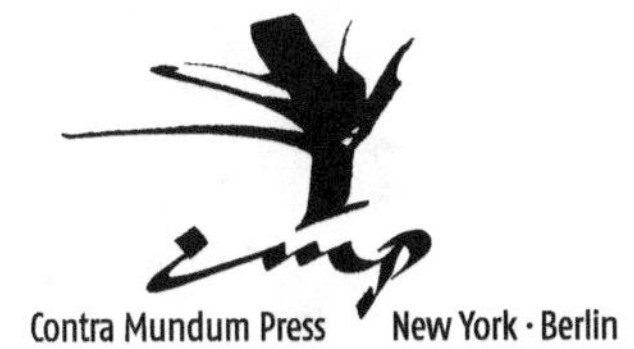

Contra Mundum Press New York · Berlin

Plays with Films

First Contra Mundum Press Edition 2013.

Library of Congress Cataloguing-in-Publication Data

Foreman, Richard, 1937–

[Plays with Films.]
Plays with Films / Richard Foreman; Edited by Rainer J. Hanshe; Introduction by George Hunka; Book design & typesetting by Alessandro Segalini

—1st Contra Mundum Press Edition
324 pp., 7 x 10 in.

ISBN 9780983697282

I. Foreman, Richard.
II. Title.
III. Hanshe, Rainer J.
IV. Editor.
V. Hunka, George.
VI. Introduction.
VII. Segalini, Alessandro.
VIII. Book design & typesetting.

2013935003

Table of Contents

INTRODUCTION

A Face that's Always the Same Face: Richard Foreman & the Projected Image

George Hunka

The three texts collected in this volume, *Zomboid!* (Film/Performance Project №1), *Wake Up Mr. Sleepy! Your Unconscious Mind is Dead!,* and *Deep Trance Behavior in Potatoland* (A Richard Foreman Theater Machine), constitute a body of formal experimentation with which Richard Foreman's Ontological-Hysteric Theater concluded its residence at the St. Mark's Church in-the-Bowery in New York. Largely eschewing the projected image in most of his past plays, Foreman integrated the projected digital image into these unique works, described by their creator as "film/performance projects" or "theater machines" instead of plays. So far as this integration constituted a response to new theater technologies then at hand, it also constituted Foreman's attempt to come to terms with the image-world of the 21st century, and the challenges to traditional consciousness and subjectivity that it presented.

Foreman had worked with projected images in the past – in the theater with *Film is Evil, Radio is Good* (1987), and in the film medium itself with his feature *Strong Medicine* (1979) – but had resisted the temptation to work with it again until digital technology added a further dimension to the projected image. The imperfections introduced into the filmic image by the mechanics of film itself – the scratches and dirt that collect on the celluloid print of the projected image over time, for example, a frequent subject of the American avant-garde filmmakers among whom Foreman had begun his theatrical career in the 1960s – were now eliminated from the experience of visual spectatorship. The two-dimensionality of the projected digital video image, pristine and clear, undamaged through countless repetitions through the mechanical device of the projector, elicited a number of other aesthetic questions. It is impossible, for example, to tell whether these images are recorded or live, whether or not the personae of the projected image were operating in the same real time as the experience of the spectator, however far away they might be in geographical distance (on other continents entirely, in the case of these three works); the ability of these images to call attention to themselves constituted a challenge not only to the aura of the reproduced artwork that Benjamin had investigated but also to the aura of the reproduced body as presented to the distant spectator, and by extension our own bodies in this arena of projected images.

The nameless live performer/characters who mediated the experience of these projections for the spectator of these works presented an often comic meditation on our own desire to become a part of this projected world – to become two-dimensional ourselves. They also demonstrated the extent to which we give up perceptual freedom as we chain ourselves to the unswerving rigidity of the digitally recorded image: both director and performers respond to the recorded image as to a click-track, an unerring and unforgiving metronome of recorded experience which does not care whether we are there or not. Whether this image-world constitutes a means of a new perceptual, social, and political autonomy or a new, unforgiving barrier to this autonomy, remains an issue that is central to the reception of all three of these works.

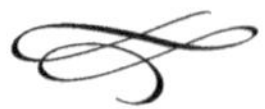

"There must be something wrong with a face that's always the same face."

Zomboid! (Film/Performance Project № 1) tries to come to terms with the projected moving image, especially as it affects stage-bound meditations on perception, and Foreman seems to have hit on a new physiological solution. The window downstage right, the window from Maria del Bosco's atelier, is back, a hole in the wall that allows the world's light to stream in as the world's light streams into the eye. Now, though, this seen world is reflected back to the audience and into the interior of *Zomboid!*'s world itself: a world of upper-middle-class interiors and individuals, a world, seen from the chaotic arena of the interior, which might indeed be upside-down: video projection as a digital retina. It's this world which the individuals of the play need to contend with and interpret now, and as that "#1" in the subtitle of *Zomboid!* indicates, this interpretation requires yet another new start.

There's nothing obscure about the objects scattered on the stage at the beginning of the show: large eyeballs & lettered blocks introduce the thematic concerns of *Zomboid!* The two other objects with which the characters need to contend during the show are the blindfold and the donkey, a "beast of burden." Fortunately, the Girl in the Beret, who is making the effort to find a purchase for herself in this world, is assisted by three other women and a tall man, who demonstrate for her the ways in which both the blindfold and the donkey can be manipulated to her own interpretive ends. The blindfold is an indication of sexual and perceptive vulnerability, but in this vulnerability is potential interpretive power: the possibility of seeing the world anew; after all, under a blindfold the eyes don't cease to function, and she indeed sees something; what each of us sees when blindfolded will be different for each of us, a play of color, an imagining of the world we can't see and over which, therefore, we have full interpretive range.

Most of the comedy of *Zomboid!* appears in the guise of the poor stuffed donkeys, which provide multiple prods to interpretation. As a metaphor for our own human bodies, the donkey is certainly a burdensome if inescapable part of our perceptions: poorly conceived vehicles for "racing" (both the human race and the rat race), but also, in one of the coarser jokes of the production, a vehicle for sex, for our personifications of Eros. Whether we saddle up our donkeys or the donkeys saddle up us is a central question in *Zomboid!* The teachers of the Girl in the Beret counsel recognition, integration, and play, which may be the wisest choice.

In *Zomboid!*, Foreman strikes out on a new humanistic road following the pessimism of his previous play, the elegiac *The Gods Are Pounding My Head!* As if he had reached the end of a road with that production, he and his theater needed to begin again, and though only a few of his former design & aesthetic approaches were abandoned, the addition of video introduced a new exterior world into this perceiver's world: it suggests a new attempt to come to terms with the social world outside the theater, a newly-recognized antagonism, and a suggestion that liberation from externally-constructed realities is still possible if only we, as perceivers, learn to begin again as well.

The play ends on a note of a new beginning. Perceptually illiterate at the start, the Girl in the Beret learns through the process not to see the world through Foreman's eyes, but through her own as she, a contemporary version of Vermeer's *A Girl Reading a Letter by an Open Window*, sits at the hole to the world, looking out, examining with confidence her own communication to herself in the light of the world, as earlier she had learned to write, to make her own symbols, with confidence and considerable beauty. (The reference to Vermeer is no mistake: the 17th-century Dutch painter's bright, unique lead-tin yellow is also used in several of the costumes worn by actors in the video.) It's an unusually peaceful, emotionally moving moment: an image of serene empowerment.

"If happiness enfolded human beings, then human beings would find it difficult to improve themselves."

"The invention of the airplane, a mortal blow to the unconscious," a deep voice says at the beginning of *Wake Up Mr. Sleepy! Your Unconscious Mind Is Dead!* As the technology of flight (and technology in general) robbed the 20th century of a dream of flight by making it physically possible, a dream fulfilled but unsatisfying in its fulfillment, the century has had to recover the dream of flight, and perhaps dreaming itself, amidst a technology of images that threatened to render dreaming and the unconscious itself superfluous.

In *Mr. Sleepy*, an aviator attempts to manipulate those remaining on the ground in a landscape newly shorn of the ability to dream, and he fails more often than he succeeds. The girls, somehow, manage to regain this ability first (perhaps it's the sensual fertility of women, of which we're reminded by the babies and their worn stuffed animals on stage, and often in their own hands), but it's not gender that's important: it's the ability to see anew, to waken what technology (or, rather, our submission to technology, since technology has no conscious will of its own) has put to sleep; to tear the newspapers (filled with useless information gathered from around the globe) wrapped around our heads to see what lies beyond them. To regain a childlike wonder, we need to become as children again.

Or we risk missing the point. Foreman's plays are completely devoid of subtext; they're all surface. "Ok, ok, are there any young children in the audience tonight?" a deep voice asks 23 seconds into the play. "If there were young children here tonight I would now be explaining to them specifically. Everything here is just for you." These are such shallow thoughts that even young children can understand them without trying; the play contains its explanation within itself. The unhappy adults of the play, the languid actors and actresses of the video presentation, grouse and complain about their situation: "Maybe it could happen in my lifetime, tick tock, tick tock; it's broken and it can't be fixed," they repeat to themselves, having given up. The unhappy children left on the ground are fearful and anxious, and much of the first half of the play is spent in seeming flight (pun intended) from the airplane that hovers above. Finally, a girl in a pantsuit begins to climb a wall and finds that, without technology, through a movement and placement of the body, a new perspective on the world can be recaptured.

Midway through the play, the adults on screen are impelled toward hope as an escape from their unhappiness: "Maybe it could happen in my lifetime," an on-screen character says. The deep voice provides, with hindsight, the antecedent to this "it" with an instruction to the children onstage and in the audience: "When the unconscious is dead the fighter airplanes say we are alone on earth, we are blind, we are deaf, with no tactile sensation. (If it is broken, if it is broken.) When the unconscious is dead please use the human mind to dig up from the depths that mental baffle machine, uncovering the sleepy giant whose name must never be spoken. (Never spoken.)" – a reach for a Judaic G-d. But the sleepy giant of our unconscious begins to be personated in our selves. On screen and on stage, the human body's sensuousness begins to be explored: a woman's bare leg is slowly caressed, the woman's face, turned toward the audience, begins to register a subtle pleasure. The world can even learn from the dream: a woman rubs her belly, slowly and thoughtfully, on screen; a girl before us imitates her action, a soothing, calming gesture that wakens the body and the unconscious alike.

Foreman's brand of political and cultural didacticism is crystal clear in *Mr. Sleepy*. "Remember, things bite back. Risk it," a voice implores. "If there were young children here tonight, I would now be explaining to them specifically that once upon a time a lonely man cried out." The voice finds, in a memory of childhood, a means of negotiating technology to find human connection again:

"Guess what it really happened to me when I was a kid. I was a young person dreaming and I climbed out of a pit in this dream, a pit dug into the earth, and as I climbed out of the pit, and looked over the edge of the pit, there over my head was an airplane flying low, and in that airplane were people, people looking at me, people jammed into the cockpit looking at me, and from their eyes, from their eyes into my body."

This could be an intense glare of belonging, of love. (And hence a woman's voice [the voice of Foreman's partner, Kate Manheim, who returns in recorded presence after some years of absence from Foreman's plays]: "... no distinction is made between ideas that are good for you, and ideas that are bad for you.")

One needs to be a young child again, a boy or a girl, to make a new beginning beyond the cultural moralisms dictated by ideas of "good for you" and "bad for you." An Eden is recaptured; as one of the screen legends has it at the very end of the play, these are "THINGS HIDDEN SINCE ... THE BEGINNING OF THE WORLD"– that is, our beginning, the world into which we are thrust at birth. Theodor Adorno, at the end of his life, posited all of his own work as an attempt to recapture his childhood, and through it, the primal source of our origin. This means recognizing the world, and all the things in it, as having emerged from that same origin: technology, the human-built screen to blind us to it. Ironically, all we need do to recapture the unconscious is to see the conscious world true. If all this seems too much to handle, Foreman holds our hand in a program note:

> "RELAX! Do not work overly hard trying to understand. Know instead it's about the elusive Unconscious Mind. Surfacing and re-surfacing (as in music). Just stay alert and notice everything that arises and asks to be 'noticed.'"

As usual in Foreman's plays, there are beautiful sequences, the most beautiful here being the rejection of the suicidal impulse when it all becomes a little too much; just as the girls prepare to slit their wrists with a pair of long knives, they make the decision, instead, to live, even with the pain that this rediscovered unconscious brings them; they drape their white delicate blindfolds over the knife-points that threatened their very lives.

The piano, like the two diminutive grand pianos that dominate the stage in *Deep Trance Behavior in Potatoland* (A Richard

Foreman Theater Machine), is among musical instruments one of the most complicated and mysterious – mysterious because most mechanical. Anyone familiar with the actions the machine must make through the disciplined, trained hand of the performer to produce a sound, knows that the piano's "action" (the proper name for that mechanism) is made up, like the human hand with its bone, muscles, nerves, flesh and blood, of dozens of parts, wood, felt and steel; what's more, unlike those of the flute or the violin, the mechanism is usually invisible to both performer and audience. The mechanism, like the mechanism of consciousness, can be explained in its physical and physiological existence. But what of the sounds it makes, the dying away of the note once attacked, or the dying away of the perception once recognized? What's left after it dies? We're not in the realm of science now, but of art and philosophy.

In the first sequence of the play, a Girl in a Golden Dress walks to center stage, faces the audience, and elaborately swallows a pill – the trancelike state follows (though, according to the controlling consciousness of the play, sounding as usual through a tape, this is an odd pill: "Imagine a pill named O-X taken every day for a period of a year. And just once each day in the twenty-four hours of its effectiveness, it links the perceived data of a specific ordinary moment to universal truth."). The live performers seem to be urged to join the two-dimensional, flat characters on the screen behind them. As production intern Anna Friedlaender wrote on the production blog for the show:

> "Sarah [Dahlen jumps] at the screen, as if she was trying to enter the screenal reality (the reverse effect from the Lumiere Brothers' train). ... [The] scene is very violent (loud thuds and flashes as well as shrieks accompany each of Sarah's attempts to jump into the screen); this violence ... evokes a feeling of struggle and urgency for Sarah to enter the screens. Secondly, Sarah seems to be checking in with the audience members on whether or not she should continue trying; between every jump she looks back at the audience with a questioning face."

The tension between the two-dimensional surface of the projected image and the three-dimensional experience of the body is stretched to the breaking point, not irrelevant to Foreman's obsession with what he called "pancake people" in his "Notes on *Zomboid!*," published in the online journal *Hot Review* in 2006. In the subtitle to this play, he introduces the consciousness of travel, of the cameras and cellphones we take with us as we fly from country to country, around the world, in those airplanes that so mystified Proust (who was also memorably mystified by telephones and revolving doors). "You understand me immediately," says a Japanese woman in the video, but we can't really understand her; she's not there, available for questioning. (And she, in her body now, doesn't see us; we're watching a digital shadow, an illusory nothingness.) Like the five performers, we may take her at her word, tranquillized by our own pills – or, we can recognize that her image and sounds, as inviting as they are, aren't even the light captured by the photographic mechanism or the sound captured by an analog recording device, but only ones and zeroes. The digital video mechanism doesn't capture people; it doesn't capture light or sound either, but only numbers (and, therefore, the mysticism attached to numerology).

The mistake is in thinking that this simulacrum is reality itself, but without the mechanism to decode these numbers (like the mechanism we use to perceive the world in its three dimensions), they remain meaningless data. *Deep Trance Behavior* suggests that, as these videos & sounds are memoirs of experience, they're a far more fragile media of memory – they're an illusory world, and our immersion in it invites us to lose our own three-dimensional existence in those ones and zeroes. The lie behind these memoirs, of course, is that they're not permanent. As a record of the past, they grant the illusion of immortality for those who believe they're captured within the two-dimensional screen; and they dull us to what is possible for us, experientially, as three-dimensional, knowing beings in this comic world. We can see characters on the screen, hear them – but we cannot touch them, and they can't feel our touch.

The irrational desire for an impossible immortality, the Spanish philosopher Unamuno believed, defined the human being as a tragic figure. The illusory immortality of the screen blinds us to the very real mortality of our own bodies. In *Deep Trance Behavior* there is, for the first time in my memory of Foreman's work, a representation of death on-stage, and even a melodramatically wailing mourner. More to the point is the tableau that ends the play: as a curtain opens in the video, finally allowing metaphorical entrance to that two-dimensional realm, it's too late for the characters on stage, who are in various states of ... rest? Or something else? Foreman would have it as a state of relaxation – "The actors are simply resting" is the last legend of the play, which we read over the fallen, motionless bodies of the performers onstage. This may be true, but it also calls into consciousness the possibility that they might also be dead, and that we may be prone ourselves to make that mistake were we not reminded of the metaphorical form of the theater itself.

In watching these works play, we are invited to become aware of our own machinery of consciousness – to recognize the two-dimensionality of the screened world, whether it's Japanese or English, as an invitation to escape our own three-dimensional, fleshed, very mortal bodies; and to recognize the tricks that these numbers play on our senses. And in this is a form of hope (Foreman is a comic, not a tragic, dramatist – and there's enormous comedy in *Deep Trance Behavior*, not to mention the showman-like flourishes for which he's known; Foreman's always had a lot of Belasco in him). The irony of mortality can be a comic irony as well as a tragic one. It's for us to decide, and recognize, as the play's own musing consciousness says:

"Do not dismiss, please, the possibility that very soon, one evening in this series of evenings, it may happen that a single individual, present at this very performance may, he or she, lock into the evening's formal fluctuations."

ZOMBOID!

(Film/Performance Project №1)

PRODUCTION HISTORY

Zomboid! (Film / Performance Project № 1). Produced by the Ontological-Hysteric Theater at the Ontological at St. Mark's Theater, New York City. January 12 – April 9, 2006. Written, directed, & designed by Richard Foreman. Video Engineering by Vivian Wenli Lin.

NYC LIVE CAST

Katherine Brook
Temple Crocker
Ben Horner
Caitlin McDonough-Thayer
Stephanie Silver

MELBOURNE FILM CAST

Görkem Acaroğlu
Margaret Cameron
Tayla Chalef
Martyn Coutts
Olivia Crang
Tara Daniel
Sue Ingleton
Kibby McKinnon
Joe Mitchell
Merfyn Owens
Rochelle Whyte
Tom Papathanassiou
Kelly Somes
Sam Strong
Willoh Weiland
Lucy Wilson

AUTHOR'S NOTE

Notes on my next project, *ZOMBOID!*

Amongst the many possible strategies of "spectator oriented" art – two seem to me to stand out. In one style – the spectator is carried on a rollercoaster through various pre-determined emotional focal points. In the second, more meditative style, events are slowed up and relatively detached from each other so the spectator can project his or her own depths, resonating with the presented "material."

ZOMBOID! (Film/Performance Project №1)

partakes of these two strategies simultaneously, with live action visceral involvement in counterpoint to on-screen projections of a more meditative nature – the actual aesthetic "event" arising in the elusive psychic space "BETWEEN" these two contrasting styles.

ZOMBOID! is the first manifestation of the International Bridge Project. A completely new venture for me – in The International Bridge Project, along with collaborator Sophie Haviland, I not only film material around the world to serve as continual "bas-relief" backdrop to my performances – but I also explore an unusual aesthetic procedure.

It is not unique that *ZOMBOID!* utilizes continual projected background for a performance event.

WHAT IS UNIQUE

is that that background is a self-contained full-length digital film, with the live performance orchestrated in front of that film, using the self-contained film as a theatrical score against which the performance is adjusted and articulated.

The performance of *ZOMBOID!* presents people responding to, echoing, and being "infected" by projected on-screen manifestations, in much the same way that in "real" life we are all psychically invaded by the many levels of material that flash in and out of the consciousness that seeds that great psychic ocean inside of which we drift.

The film itself is meditative, non-narrative, beautiful and somewhat off-kilter – yet containing no "extraordinary events."

NO EXTRAORDINARY EVENTS?

Again and again these days I see films and plays being promoted to audiences on the basis of the many "interesting" real-life subjects presented in those works.

It seems we live in a world where everyone is interested above all else in "interesting subjects." But shockingly – I maintain, that the desire for subjects of "interesting subject matter" is, in fact, an avoidance of the REAL subject of real art, which is – What?

The real subject is presence itself, the scintillating "presence," of any and all selected items – but presented in such a way that one's primary experience (the aesthetic experience) is to realize that the SUBJECT ITSELF doesn't matter – but is always in fact the TRIVIAL aspect of the art event.

That trivial aspect (the "subject") is what we focus on when we choose NOT to be deeply engaged with what art is deeply about – the full, multi-dimensional "presence" of whatever subject is being obliterated by the power of "present-ness." However, by the usual gluing of our attention onto the ostensible "subject matter" – we try to protect ourselves from the deep ego-shattering experience of art.

Oh, you say – but Shakespeare had stories and subjects! Yes – but we've had it, and had it, and had it *ad infinitum* – and now we are into something else – new, adventurous, rewarding and full of delight in unexpected ways. But, you say – Shakespeare (for instance) had stories PLUS a poetry that fragmented simple coherence with a wide range of associative mental links. But I maintain that now the time is ripe for other strategies in the midst of this floundering and spiritually confused world.

IN FACT

much to my surprise, I began this work believing I was entering a new realm of art-making – and that with *ZOMBOID!* I was entering a realm of pure aesthetics – but as I started putting down my thoughts – describing to myself and to others what I believe I am doing in this work – I realized a certain ANGER rising in me, and I realized I was thinking more in political terms than I had expected. (The politics of art-making, certainly).

I REALIZED THAT I BELIEVE, THAT NOW IS THE TIME FOR A CELEBRATION OF ELITIST ART!

Let's dare proclaim that in the face of a society increasingly crying for a media-driven, market-oriented, popular art, reaching out to everyone at once – while "deep thoughts" are officially allowed in such art, they must only come in a form that is easily communicable to all.

BUT I MAINTAIN

that to feed the individual human spirit, the true art of these times must be a kind of demanding gymnasium where sensibilities get rigorous exercise – so that those sensibilities then become more refined, able to pick up on and appreciate the patterned intricacies of a world which is usually, in art, simplified into recognizable social and psychological clichés or knock-out effects. Such normal strategies lie about the world because they talk about what we already know (which is always wrong) in languages with which we are already familiar (and therefore put our more delicate mental mechanisms to sleep) – all this, instead of waking us up with the uncharted energies that throb behind the facade of the shared world of communicable convention.

SO IN TODAY'S ARENA, I MAINTAIN THAT ONLY ELITIST ART

presents the true facts of "always-in-process" human beings who, while pretending to themselves and others that they are coherent "wholes" – are really but a tissue of micro-tendencies and impulses, most of which are effectively ignored by the defense mechanism of consciousness that allows the individual to feel secure in his or her "picture of the world."

BUT ELITIST ART

offers the spectator a chance, through the development of subtle discriminations, to enter the true PARADOX of lucid, aesthetic sensibility.

ELITIST ART

"trumps" the popular art of media culture, offering the alternative to the bottom-line world that leaves so many of us parched, spiritually depleted, half-human precisely because we are asked –

TO DENY OUR ELITIST TENDENCIES!

NOW – ANYBODY IS WELCOME TO ENJOY ELITIST ART.

It tends to speak of powerful hidden things and energies, in language (the full range of theatrical language) that is isomorphic with those hidden things and energies, rather than in the language of daily life – because a language made isomorphic with such intuited processes seems most connected to ultimate, deep-lying things.

AND TO POINT TOWARD THOSE ULTIMATE THINGS

in the case of this performance – *ZOMBOID!*, the motif utilized is

THE BLINDFOLD.

How does this work? The aesthetic goal in *ZOMBOID!* is to build an entire world from small image/idea clusters that bounce off other image/idea clusters – much like the way the real world is generated from millions of small, local interactions between event quanta from different realms.

The performance of *ZOMBOID!* is then an attempted model of the depth of the world at work.

The world, it would seem, starts out not with a story or a theme, but with the random (statistically guided, perhaps) pouring forth of multitudinous radiations – twitching and throbbing in concert.

So now, here in front of an audience – we invoke & mirror this world process, generating the energy of eternal delight.

Required of us all, however, in order to be sensitive and alert to what is invisibly taking place in the depths of the world's creativity, is to free ourselves from both perceptual habit and inherited mental habit. (Keatsean "negative capability.")

One must, in effect, blindfold oneself, blocking normal faculties so that other inner resources are forced into play.

The theme of the blindfold becomes, then, the theme of "in-sight."

But an insight that produces not "ideas," because ideas, no matter how convincing, are never more than the tiniest slice of the full pie of reality and, therefore, always less than the whole truth.

Instead, we would, through aesthetic means, rhythm and composition, event and paradox – "tune" the deep self to the "truth" that all things echo and reflect all other things. We would work toward the perspective that each isolated moment, even those that seem relatively empty, is in fact pulsating with the full energy of the deep source, and so, the motif of *ZOMBOID!* is the facilitating

BLINDFOLD!

But in *ZOMBOID!*, the embodiment of that motif generates a unique "No Man's Land" between two aesthetic worlds presented simultaneously on-stage.

THE STAGE IS SPLIT

between the meditative world of archetypal TABLEAUX, (imaginary "mental" content projected on screen) – and in counterpoint – the concrete world of physical bodies, twisting and lurching in reaction to irrational impulses that "trump" the myths & hierarchies of consciousness that we normally believe organize human life.

THE UNBRIDGEABLE SPLIT

between these two worlds is the "location" in which *ZOMBOID!* manifests itself. The art event is, then, a new and unnamable "thing" that arises in the space between screen image and live bodies – a space that is intuited rather than seen & identified.

To risk offering an art based on this "split" is to walk the tightrope over the abyss between imagined human mastery and the un-chartable "other" that is never controllable or knowable.

– BALANCING PRECARIOUSLY

in that energized limbo where the art called "difficult" does its secret and unpredictable work.

STORIES HIDE THE TRUTH

Richard Foreman's new work is based on projected images, but NOT because he accepts the proposition that this technological form should now take center stage in our current version of reality.

He rejects such an idea. Rather – he places slow, tableau-like projected images at the center of these productions because they are able to ground the "Reality" of the live performance which occurs in front of these images, in the hallucinatory temporal coagulation of time passing – evoked in projected symbolic tableaux that do not so much "advance," but rather breathe, drift, & palpitate, just like the world around us is quietly doing while our limited mental faculties agitatedly invent adventures and interpretations we project as our daily reality – but which in fact exists under that atmospheric blanket of the "GREATER" reality which is the slow oscillation of the cosmic drift.

So the projected images in Foreman's new work certainly do not point toward a commitment to the new and superficial technological society, but rather to the slow evolution of cosmic forces, massively coagulating into images & symbols behind our backs, that used to be called, dare we say it ... God.

ZOMBOID!

(Film/Performance Project №1)

The stage is a large room with one projection screen on the upstage wall and another on the stage-left wall joined at a 60° angle. At the base of each screen about four feet from the ground is a ledge upon which rest numerous objects, including small framed photos, vases, lettered cubes, & small toys. In addition, small panels, each containing a single light bulb, are located at the bottom left corner of each screen – when opened, these generate flares of light across each respective screen and into the stage area. Along the edges of the screen on the upstage wall are two small electric candelabras. Throughout the play, the same film is projected on each screen. The printed words or phrases that appear on the screen throughout the play indicated in the following texts by large capital letters typically remain present for a brief period of time and then vanish.

Several thin wires crisscross the stage horizontally at different heights and distances. There are also two four-foot high plexiglass walls running from downstage right to downstage center and from downstage left to downstage center, with a small open partition between them. There is a two-inch black-and-white vertically striped runner that stretches across the top of the plexiglass. A small ledge atop the plexiglass wall is lined with toy army soldiers, evenly distributed, each facing the audience. At various intervals along the plexiglass are flat rectangular light bulbs turned toward the audience; at different times throughout the performance, they flash on & off.

Other objects are scattered around the stage including books, a small settee, several black chairs with red cushions, rattles, scepters, sledgehammers, ritualistic wands, vases, urns. Upstage right there is a large black clocktower-like object. It rests on a platform with wheels, has slabs of fake rock around its circular base, and is topped with a green pyramid.

Each of its four sides has a round red dial without numbers or clock arms. The clocktower object is wheeled in and out at various moments throughout the performance and each empty clockface is sometimes illuminated by a revolving light bulb at its center. Three giant eyeballs with Hebrew letters circling the iris are placed about the stage; they are often carried aloft by the actors, or rolled along the stage floor.

The floor is flat black, like a chalkboard, and has white lines running across it as well as a thick red stripe crossing it diagonally that connects to a red stripe that runs along the stage-left wall; one more red stripe runs along the upstage wall to the side of the screen. There are also numerous stretches of short black pipe that vertically line part of the stage, like short hurdles. Parts of the walls are covered with illegible words in chalk. At stage right, there are three four-foot-high black partitions with curved tops; above them is a large open window. At center stage, a soft life-size baby donkey is lying on its side on the ground. There is black electrical tape wound around the center of its stomach and at three different intervals on each leg.

Typesetting Key

`00:00 (time stamp)`

SCREEN — Screen tableaux

SCREEN LEGENDS

Live stage action

`Voiceover`

Sound & Music cue

`raised-hyphen: word pronounced with elongated syllables`

0:00 FACES – spring morning: close-up of woman with short hair standing outside. She stares into the camera. From time to time, she blinks and winces.

Sound cue: *plastic drum.*

1:34 FACES – spring morning: left-wipe to close-up of dour-faced woman with long hair standing outside. She stares into the camera.

Ben, a man dressed in black with a white ski cap, walks to center stage. He stares at the upstage screen, then crosses under the wires, walks in a circular motion, exits stage left.

2:06 FACES – spring morning: left-wipe to close-up of an old, bald, bearded man's face. He is standing outside against a wall with crumbling paint. He stares into the camera.

Stephanie enters from stage right carrying a stuffed donkey on her back. She walks to center stage and sits on top of another stuffed donkey.

While crouched behind a black partition, CAITLIN & TEMPLE point their fingers toward the donkey and whisper in unison in falsetto: "Look at Ste-pha-nie. Ste-pha-nie's car-ry-ing a don-key. Thirty-seven times. [Sound cue: *plastic drum.*] Ste-pha-nie's carrying a don-key. Ste-pha-nie's car-ry-ing the same damn don-key."

2:40 FACES – spring morning: left-wipe to close-up of a young man with a mustache standing against the wall with crumbling paint. He stares into the camera.

Katherine, Caitlin, and Temple enter from stage right and stand in front of the plexiglass wall with their arms crossed facing the upstage screen.

Deep Voice: `Sup-pose. Sup-pose.`

Music cue: *discordant piano & violin.*

Stephanie removes the donkey from her back then turns and faces the upstage screen. Ben walks off stage while Katherine, Caitlin, and Temple walk to center stage and kneel before the donkey. They ceremoniously place their hands around a scepter, which they hold over the donkey, then flip through little red books, which they sometimes hold up to their faces to cover their eyes.

Deep Voice: `Well.`

3:08

POSTULATE ?

FACES – spring morning: left-wipe to close-up of young woman with short hair standing outside. She stares into the camera. From time to time, she blinks.

Katherine, Caitlin, Temple, and Stephanie stare at the upstage screen.

3:43 **FACES** – spring morning: left-wipe to close-up of woman with shoulder-length dark hair standing outside. She stares into the camera.

Deep Voice: `Don-key.`

Light flare washes out the screen.

Sound cue: *chime.*

Deep Voice: Don-key.

3:58 **FACES** – spring morning: left-wipe to close-up of the same woman. She looks down, then back up.

Katherine, Caitlin, Temple, and Stephanie return to reading through their red books, then turn and stare at the audience.

Voice: a professor lecturing on Beethoven in German.

4:25 **FACES** – spring morning: left-wipe to close-up of woman with greenish-yellow beret and red lipstick. She stares into the camera.

Female Voice: Chan-te a-vec moi.

SUPPOSE ?

Sound cue: *donkey hee-haw (3x).*

Deep Voice: Don-key.

All of the actresses lift their hands to cover their faces.

Voice: a professor lecturing on Beethoven in German.

4:55 **FACES** – spring morning: left-wipe to man with short hair standing outside. He stares into the camera.

5:02 **FACES** – spring morning: left-wipe to the same man. Screen flare.

Sound cue: *shattering glass, bell.*

The actresses all rise – Stephanie moves to stage left and stares at the screen; Katherine and Caitlin move to upstage center and stare at the upstage screen. Temple walks to stage right and climbs on top of one of the black partitions and stares into a large open window. Ben carries an object draped in black cloth to center stage.

Deep Voice (singing with strong emphasis on each syllable): `They do it on a don-key. They do it in a hole in the wall. They do it where they find me hi-ding.`

5:36 **TABLEAU – left-wipe to a group of men and women, some of whom are blindfolded, clustered together in a dark room, some sitting, some standing.**

Deep Voice: `The (Sup-pose) best of all. (Sup-pose.)`

Stephanie wraps a blindfold around her eyes as Katherine wraps a blindfold around Caitlin. Temple comes down from the partition and lies on the ground. Ben turns in a circle with the covered object then walks off stage.

TABLEAU – GIRL in blindfold: "Suppose I were to postulate ..."

Sound cue: *clicking noise (2x).*

Deep Voice (drawn out): `Please.`

Screen flare.

TABLEAU – GIRL in blindfold: "... that those things never under control, are under control, backwards. How would you deal with that?"

6:29 **TABLEAU – left-wipe to washout of screen and then to previous scene.**

Stephanie carries one of the stuffed donkeys to stage right and places it on top of Temple. Caitlin rolls one of the Giant Eyeballs next to the donkey then lifts it up and places it on top of the donkey. The iris faces the audience. Stephanie and Katherine come and stand behind Caitlin.

Deep Voice: `Rule.`

Light flare washes out the screen.

Ben walks to the donkey, removes it from under the Eyeball, then places it against the stage-left wall.

Sound cue: *loud clicking noise (3x).*

Deep Voice (winding down): `Rule. 1, 2, 3, 4, 5.`

Bulb flash.

7:45 **TABLEAU – Blindfolded GIRL (while a man in a suit whispers into her ear): "Suppose I were to postulate ..."**

Deep Voice: `Please.`

TABLEAU – Blindfolded GIRL: "... that those things never under control, are under control, backwards. How would you deal with that?"

Stephanie removes the Eyeball from Temple, holds it above her head, then leans backwards with it, freezes, then runs off stage.

Deep Voice: Please.

8:15

HIDING?

Deep Voice: 1, 2, 3, 4, 5.

Temple gingerly picks up a four-squared lettered wooden block, [**bulb flash**] walks stage left, bends over, turns the block upside down, places it against her face. She hands it to Ben, who is crouched under the stage-left screen, turns toward the audience, then walks upstage, retrieves another four-squared lettered wooden block from the ledge under the screen and hands it to Katherine, who is also crouched under the stage-left screen. Katherine examines the object, turning it about, then places it on the ledge above her.

Sound cue: *clicking noise (2x).*

Bulb flash.

Female Voice: Ex-per-ience.

TABLEAU – MAN: "If you were to postulate ... that those things never under control –"

Deep Voice: Nor-mal.

TABLEAU – MAN, continuing: "are under control, backwards. I would have to deal with that."

Sound cue: *clicking noise (2x).*

Bulb flash.

Temple walks to center stage and kicks a pillow.

Sound cue: *shattering glass.*

A light beams toward Temple from the stage-right wall. She walks toward it, then climbs a small ladder and stares into the window from which the light is projected, then back toward the screen.

9:11 **TABLEAU – the blindfold is removed from the girl.**

Music cue: *gentle melodic tune with vocal in French.*

Deep Voice: `Sup-pose.`

Female Voice: `Chan-te a-vec moi. Chan-te a-vec moi.`

Deep Voice: `Sup-pose. [Singing, with strong emphasis on each syllable.] They do it on a don-key.`

TABLEAU – WOMAN: "Suppose I were to postulate ... those things never under control, are under control, backwards. How would you deal with that?"

Deep Voice (singing with strong emphasis on each syllable): `They do it in a hole in the wall. They do it where they find me hi-ding.`

Sound cue: *computerized swooshing noise (3 x).*

Stephanie opens a panel in the bottom left corner of the upstage screen.

10:05 **TABLEAU** – MAN: "That those things never under control, are under control, backwards. I would have to deal with that."

Deep Voice (singing with strong emphasis on each syllable): `The best of all. BUT best of all, they are go-ing to do it. They are go-ing to do it.`

Light flare on upstage screen.

TABLEAU – the girl is blindfolded again.

10:38

Female Voice: `Chan-te a-vec moi.`

Temple opens a panel on the stage right screen. She stares into the two glaring lights, then covers her eyes.

Sound cue: *computerized swooshing noise (3x).*

Deep Voice: `1, 2, 3, 4, 5.`

Bulb flash.

Sound cue: *clicking noise.*

Light flare in screen panels dies out.

Female Voice: `Chan-te a-vec moi.`

Music cue: *modernist piano excerpt.*

BEN: Don't move, don-key.

Deep Voice: `Re-min-der.`

Temple and Katherine close the screen panels.

Female Voice: Chan-te a-vec moi.

Sound cue: *computerized swooshing noise (3x).*

Female Voice: Chan-te a-vec moi.

11:35

Deep Voice: Be-hav-ior.

> **TABLEAU 2** — left-wipe to blindfolded girl and several people in a room staring out windows. Left-wipe to the very same scene. Merv rises & stares out a window.

Female Voice: Ex-per-ience.

Deep Voice: Once on-ly.

> All of the actors stand before the screens and stretch their arms toward them.
>
> Light flare on screens. All of the actors wince. Ben and Stephanie point at one another and run around each other in a circle.
>
> CAITLIN / TEMPLE: 1, 2, 3.
>
> All of the stage actors sit under the screen ledges then fall to the ground and screech.

Deep Voice: A lifetime is an accurate di-ag-no-sis. [Sound cue: *soft gong*] Ac-cur-ate.

Music cue: *soft violin.*

12:35

REMINDER?

Music: *gentle melodic tune with vocal in French.*

Bulb flash (3x).

12:50

Music cue: *eerie noises.*

SUPPOSE?

Bulb flash.

TABLEAU 2 – GIRL in blindfold: "Suppose I were to postulate, one must swallow reality –"

Deep Voice: `Pri-vate (Pri-vate) performance.`

13:06 TABLEAU 2 – left-wipe to the same room.

Ben lifts a stuffed donkey into the air and throws it upstage.

13:12 TABLEAU 2 – left-wipe to the same room. During this sequence, a woman continues to circle around the blindfolded girl.

BEN: Don't move, don-key.

Deep Voice: `Don-key.`

The actors bring empty picture frames to center stage and hold them above the stuffed donkey.

TEMPLE / CAITLIN (slowly elongating each number in a whisper): 1, 2, 3.

Stephanie enters carrying a sword in each hand & walks to the group of actors seated around the donkey, then proceeds to the stage-right wall and leans against it, gazing at the stage-left screen.

Music cue: *haunting violin & clarinet.*

Female Voice (increasing in volume): `Chan-te a-vec moi. Chan-te a-vec moi. Chan-te a-vec moi. Chan-te a-vec moi.`

Deep Voice: `Pri-vate.`

Music: *modernist angular piano excerpt.*

TABLEAU – Merv turns away from the window and toward the camera, staring directly into it.

Sound cue: *computer blip, wood block.*

Deep Voice: `In-ev-i-ta-ble.`

Caitlin walks to stage right and stands against one of the partitions and stares at Stephanie, then turns toward the stage-left screen, then toward the upstage screen.

Music cue: *haunting violin.*

Voice: `a professor lecturing in German on Beethoven.`

`15:20`

INEVITABLE?

Ben, Caitlin, and Temple stare at the upstage screen.

Deep Voice: Why not?

Music cue: *modernist angular piano & violin.*

Caitlin turns toward the audience, then, slowly, back toward the upstage screen.

Deep Voice: Why not – PLEASE – take [sound cue: *soft gong*] the fun out of LIFE – ex-per-i-ence a true – stretch of time.

16:08 **TABLEAU 2 – GIRL in blindfold: "Suppose I were to postulate ... that one must swallow reality in order to produce accurate mental copies [screen flare out;** sound cue: *shattering glass* **] of that same reality.** [Sound cue: *shattering glass*] **How would you deal with that?"**

Bulb flash.

Deep Voice: Su-ch an 'ea-sy game' – BECAUSE – [sound cue: *chime*] (Ac-cur-ate) – there are no rules to this game.

Bulb flash.

All of the actors scream.

16:56 Katherine, standing center stage with her arms outstretched, holds a ten-inch-high stuffed strawberry in her hands, bottom up. Ben is pointing a gun at her. Temple and Stephanie run toward Ben & Katherine with swords.

Sound cue: *clicking noise (2x).*

Deep Voice: `Three, four, five.`

Caitlin and Katherine gingerly walk away with the stuffed strawberry then turn and stare at the upstage screen while continuing to hold the strawberry.

Deep Voice: `One, two, three, four, five.`

TABLEAU 2 – a woman removes the blindfold from the girl in the center.

Deep Voice: `Sup-pose. Sup-pose I were to pos-tu-late –`

Bulb flash; screen flare.

Music cue: *screeching violin.*

Sound cue: *scraping noise.*

All of the actors remain still and stare at the audience.

17:40

SUPPOSE?

Caitlin and Katherine gingerly place the strawberry on the ground.

TABLEAU 2 – GIRL (turns to camera): "If one were to postulate one must swallow reality in order to produce accurate mental copies of that same reality, then I would have to deal with that."

Music cue: *fast violin.*

17:58

REMINDER?

Sound cue: *scraping noise.*

18:10

DO NOT TOUCH?

Deep Voice: Why not – PLEASE – take the fun out of LIFE – Ex-per-i-ence.

Sound cue: *bell.*

Bulb flash.

Caitlin picks up the stuffed strawberry and gingerly holds it before her. Katherine takes it from her and cradles it in her arms.

18:32

DO NOT TOUCH?

Stephanie blindfolds Caitlin.

Sound cue: *scraping noise continues.*

Bulb flash.

18:49 **TABLEAU 3 – three people seated around a table in a tiled room: one is blindfolded and another wears a yellow turban. Behind them is a man standing on another table; in front of them are two blindfolded people.**

Temple places a small stack of books under the stuffed strawberry in Katherine's hands, then walks away.

Deep Voice: `In-ev-i-ta-ble.`

Katherine drops the books and the strawberry. Temple runs in to retrieve them. Caitlin lifts her hands to her breasts as Katherine runs behind her and puts her hands over her eyes.

Bulb flash.

Voice: `Va-voom. Va-voom.`

TABLEAU 2 – MAN: "Suppose I were to postulate – This is different. Is this different? How would you deal with that?"

Ben pulls the clocktower to center stage.

Deep Voice: `Well. Well.`

Blindfolded, Caitlin walks away. Stephanie grabs a piece of chalk and begins writing on the base of the clocktower. Katherine pretends to strike the clocktower with a sledgehammer. Temple watches Caitlin remove her blindfold and place it on the ground between the black metal piping. Caitlin wraps her feet and hands around the piping.

Caitlin rises and walks to center stage with a red book as Ben places an object inside the base of the clocktower. Opening her book, Caitlin turns toward the audience as if to speak, opening her mouth, but remains silent. Stephanie continues writing on the clocktower base.

Music cue: *mournful modernist violin.*

Caitlin solemnly walks away, then kneels before Temple with the book, showing her a passage within it as Ben pulls the clocktower off stage.

Bulb flash.

20:06 Screen whited out.

Deep Voice: May-be.

TABLEAU 3 – MAN: "Suppose I were to postulate – This is different. Is this different? How would you deal with that?"

Deep Voice: Re-min-der.

Ben and Katherine move to stage right and put their forefingers to their foreheads as they stare at the upstage screen. Caitlin and Temple sit stage right, one reading a miniature book while facing the audience, the other reading a miniature book while facing the upstage screen.

Sound cue: *computer blip.*

20:42 **TABLEAU 3** – MAN: "Suppose I were to postulate – This is different."

Music cue: *mournful modernist violin, increasing in volume and then going silent.*

KATHERINE, BEN, & STEPHANIE clap their hands and shout in unison "1, 2" then point back to their heads as they stare at the upstage screen then lift their hands to their mouths, in a gesture of blessing.

TABLEAU 3 – MAN: "How would you deal with that?"

21:12 **TABLEAU 3** – girls with blindfolds exit left and right.

SUPPOSE?

Deep Voice: Well.

21:21

SUPPOSE I WERE TO POSTULATE

High-pitched Voice: Now. Now. Right now. Now. Now. Now. Now. Now. Now.

Bulb flash.

Deep Voice (overlapping): Remember – it is not possible to both look and list-en (Pos-si-ble) at the same time. Deep-ly. Well.

21:36 **TABLEAU 3** – the girls all turn toward the wall.

The actors remain still.

22:00

RULES FOR BEGINNERS?

TABLEAU 3 – the girls all turn back. The seated man is blindfolded.

Lights on the clocktower spin and spin.

Bulb flash.

Deep Voice: `Well. Take off the blin-ders.`

22:25 **TABLEAU 3** – MAN: "Suppose I were to postulate – This is different. Is this different? How would you deal with that?"

Sound cue: *eerie noise.*

Bulb flash.

Temple throws a miniature red book down on the floor. Ben picks it up and begins turning the pages. Temple takes it away from him.

22:43 **TABLEAU 3** – WOMAN: "If you were to postulate – This is different. Is this different? I would have to deal with that."

Temple spanks Stephanie with the book.

STEPHANIE: Owww.

Ben pulls a rug with armholes and jangling tassels onstage then wraps Katherine in it. Katherine puts her hands through the armholes then extends her arms directly above. Caitlin walks back and forth from stage left to stage right while counting on her fingers.

23:11 Temple carries a stuffed donkey to Katherine and places it on top of her, then sits on top of the donkey as Katherine rocks it back and forth.

TABLEAU 3 – WOMAN in yellow turban: "If you were to postulate – This is different. Is this different? I would have to deal with that."

Music cue: *modernist violin.*

Sound cue: *alarm (3x).*

Deep Voice (drawn out): `Nor-mal.`

Light bulbs at the bottom of the upstage screen flare on.

High-pitched Voice: `Ri, di di di di di di di de dooo; twee, ri di di di di di di do daaa.`

23:30

ACCURATE MENTAL COPIES?

Deep Voice: `Once on-ly. Well.`

Bulb flash.

Music cue: *repetitive industrial loop.*

TABLEAU 3 – the girls all turn away.

Deep Voice: `Well. Per-fect. Per-fect.`

TABLEAU 3 – the girls all turn back.

KATHERINE (in sing-song voice as she rocks the donkey back and forth on top of her): Don-key 1, don-key 2.

Deep Voice: `Well.`

Sound cue: *elephant roaring (3x).*

Ben slowly approaches Katherine & stands before her.

KATHERINE: Don-key 1, don-key 2, don-key 3, don-key 4, don-key 5, don-key 6, don-key 7.

24:14 **TABLEAU 3 – left-wipe to two blindfolded men: one is in a suit with a yellow tie and the other is in a black turtleneck. Behind them are several other people in blindfolds seated behind a rug.**

Ben stands over Katherine and leans back, stretches his arms out in front of himself, then slides them forwards & backwards as he turns toward the audience. She stops. He moves to Katherine's feet, does the same gesture, then stops.

Deep Voice: `That Beast of the in-ev-i-ta-ble (In-ev-i-ta-ble) – REAL burden.`

Caitlin wraps a black and white checkered sheet around herself and stares into the audience. Katherine continues to rock the donkey back and forth on her body.

24:40

INEVITABLE SHORT CIRCUIT ?

TABLEAU 3 – MAN: "Suppose I were to postulate – intensifying the hunger for information breeds total catastrophe ... How would you deal with that?"

Ben returns to Katherine's head and repeats the same gesture. Temple holds a scepter over Caitlin's head, then lightly taps her head with the object [sound cue: *ding*]. Caitlin turns toward her and begins singing in falsetto as Temple points the scepter at her like a sword. She is also singing in falsetto.

Stephanie jogs in carrying two long sticks.

CAITLIN / TEMPLE (singing in low shrill voice): Look at Ste-pha-nie. Ste-pha-nie's car-ry-ing the sticks. Thir-ty-seven times in a row, Ste-pha-nie's car-ry-ing the sticks.

Music cue: *modernist piano.*

Deep Voice: `That inevitable don-key did not (Pro-blem).`

Music cue: *screeching violin.*

Ben wraps a blindfold around his eyes, then takes the two sticks from Stephanie and places the end of one stick on the donkey's ass and the end of the other on the donkey's head.

Music cue: *modernist piano.*

25:17

'FINGERS'

Deep Voice: `Once on-ly.`

25:28

TEN 'FINGERS'

TABLEAU 4 – MAN: "Suppose I were to postulate ..."

TABLEAU 4 – wipe to the same scene and screen flare out.

Music cue: *modernist violin.*

Caitlin leans against Temple, who comforts her.

Deep Voice: `In-ev-i-ta-ble.`

Music cue: *fast harpsichord.*

High-pitched Voice: `Now, now, now.`

Screen flare.

Ben hands the sticks back to Stephanie.

High-pitched Voice: `Now, now, now.`

Ben kneels before the donkey and caresses its neck.

26:10

FORTY 'FINGERS'

TABLEAU 4 – MAN: "Suppose I were to postulate – intensifying the hunger for information breeds total catastrophe ... How would you deal with that?"

Ben retracts his hands, stares at them, then gazes at the audience.

26:24

THAT INEVITABLE DONKEY?

Deep Voice: Somebody else picks (1, 2, 3, 4, 5) up the ball, and runs with it. And does other, hard im-pos-si-ble things.

Bulb flash.

Music cue: *modernist piano & violin.*

Stephanie points the long sticks at Ben. He stops, then takes hold of the other end of each stick. Ben and Stephanie prance off stage, slowly pumping the sticks like a locomotive.

Music cue: *modernist piano, fast harpsichord.*

26:57

NO OTHER WORLD IS REAL

Bulb flash (3x).

Temple runs to center stage and kicks the donkey in the ass.

KATHERINE (as she rocks the donkey back & forth on top of her): Don-key 1, don-key 2, don-key 3, don-key 4, don-key 5.

Screen flare.

Stephanie enters and sits on top of the donkey. Temple holds her hands over Stephanie's eyes. Ben enters and blindfolds Temple.

Music cue: *fast harpsichord.*

Voice (stridently): No, no, no, you have to go back and do it again. This is not the way to do it. Believe me. This is not the way to do it. Go back! Go back!

TABLEAU 4 – MAN: "Suppose I were to postulate – intensifying the hunger for information breeds total catastrophe ... How would you deal with that?"

Voice: a professor lecturing in German on Beethoven.

27:59 **TABLEAU 4** – the blindfold is removed from the second man.

Voice: a professor lecturing in German on Beethoven continues, increasing in volume.

'DONKEY'

28:13 **TABLEAU 4** – MAN in suit with yellow tie: "If you were to postulate – intensifying the hunger for information breeds to-tal catastrophe ... I would have to deal with that."

Deep Voice (overlapping TABLEAU): 1, 2, 3, 4, 5.

Sound cue: *ringing phone.*

Ben places his hands over his eyes, then removes them and turns toward the stage-left screen and stares at it.

Voice: a professor lecturing in German on Beethoven continues, increasing in volume.

High-pitched Voice: Right now. Right now.

28:31

THAT BEAST OF / BURDEN

High-pitched Voice: Now, now, now.

Voice: a professor lecturing in German on Beethoven continues.

TABLEAU 4 – a girl wraps a blindfold around Merv's forehead, then pushes it down over his eyes.

Bulb flash.

Deep Voice: That in-ev-i-ta-ble be-hav-ior. In-ev-i-ta-ble be-hav-ior.

28:56

Sound cue: *ringing phone.*

TABLEAU 4 – the second man is blindfolded again just as was Merv. The girl walks away.

High-pitched Voice: Now, right now.

Ben removes the blindfold from Temple.

Music cue: *modernist violin.*

Stephanie pulls the donkey off Katherine, who stands up and tries to retrieve the donkey. Caitlin runs across stage and crouches down.

Bulb flash.

Voice: a professor lecturing in German on Beethoven stops.

Screen flare.

Deep Voice: Pri-vate (Pri-vate) performance.

Temple runs off stage with the donkey. Katherine and Caitlin walk toward her to try to catch her but stop, then scream in unison in falsetto as they each spin around then bump into one another and jiggle their bodies up and down.

Music cue: *gentle melodic tune with vocal in French.*

29:23

THE REAL DONKEY ?

TABLEAU 4 – MAN in yellow tie: "If you were to postulate – intensifying the hunger for information breeds total catastrophe ..."

Music cue: *gentle melodic tune with vocal in French.*

Kaitlin and Catherine stop jiggling and exit stage right and left.

Deep Voice: Rule.

TABLEAU 4 – MAN in yellow tie: "I would have to deal with that."

Temple raises a scepter in the air above her head while facing the audience.

Deep Voice: `Sup-pose.`

Sound cue: *shattering glass, eerie noise.*

29:48 **TABLEAU 5 – left-wipe and another left-wipe to several people clustered together on a stairwell, some standing, some sitting, as a blindfolded girl holds the bannister.**

Sound cue: *shattering glass, eerie noise.*

Temple holds the scepter above her head again. Ben enters with a small three-paneled billboard with a donkey on each panel, places it on the ground, opens it, then closes it quickly, holds it up and turns in different directions, displaying the donkey to everyone.

Deep Voice: `The in-ev-i-ta-ble don-key.`

TEMPLE: Fly a-way, don-key.

30:08 CAITLIN / KATHERINE: Now! Don-key time.

Sound cue: *computerized swooshing noise (3x).*

Deep Voice: `Don-key.`

KATHERINE & CAITLIN run to stage right, spit in their hands, rub them together, then each mount a separate black partition, grab the pole behind them, and chant: "1, 2, 3" as they rock the pole back and forth.

Sound cue: *shattering glass.*

Deep Voice: It would be fine in-deed if there were rules for beginners.

KATHERINE / CAITLIN (while knocking their boots and the pole against the partition): 1, 2, 3.

KATHERINE: You go!

CAITLIN: No, you go!

KATHERINE / CAITLIN: 1, 2, 3.

Sound cue: *swooshing computer noise (3x).*

TABLEAU 4 – blindfolded girl in black dress begins walking down the stairs.

Sound cue: shattering glass.

TEMPLE: Fly away dumb, mys-tic don-key peo-ple.

Voice: Bi, bi, bi, bi, beep; o-ca, o-ca, o-ca, o-ca.

30:51

Sound cue: *loud echoing scraping noise.*

TABLEAU 5 – girl in red dress with blindfold begins crawling down the stairs.

Voice (stridently): No, no, no, you have to go back and do it again. This is not the way to do it. Believe me. This is not the way to do it. Go back! Go back!

Music cue: *gentle melodic tune with vocal in French.*

31:11

SUPPOSE?

Deep Voice: Please let me in.

Bulb flash.

Sound cue: *clicking noise.*

Music cue: *modernist violin.*

31:18 **TABLEAU 5** – WOMAN: "If I were to postulate –"

KATHERINE / CAITLIN: 1, 2, 3.

TABLEAU 5 – WOMAN, continuing: "time passing."

Deep Voice: Sup-pose.

31:24

SUPPOSE I WERE TO POSTULATE

Deep Voice: Sup-pose I were to pos-tu-late.

Bulb flash.

TABLEAU 5 – wipe and tilt to the same scene.

KATHERINE / CAITLIN: Boop-i-di-boo.

Sound cue: *ringing phone, shattering glass (2x), donkey hee-haw (3x).*

Ben rushes in with a stool to center stage then falls to the ground, and drops stool.

Sound cue: *wood block.*

31:46 **TABLEAU 5 – left-wipe to the same scene.**

Temple runs to center stage, stares at the stool, then up at the stage-left screen. She picks up the stool and sets it aright.

TEMPLE: Naugh-ty.

BEN: Naugh-ty, naugh-ty.

31:53 **TABLEAU 5 – left-wipe to the same scene.**

Temple sits on the stool and blindfolds herself then places her hands behind her back. Everyone else remains still.

Sound cue: *wood block.*

32:01 Temple rises from the stool and begins to walk around. Ben wheels the clocktower to center stage.

TABLEAU 5 – blindfolded girl in black dress walks down the stairs from the top again.

Stephanie, who is wearing a black blindfold, walks along the edge of the stage-left screen, guiding herself by slowly running her hands along the ledge.

32:25 Temple rises from the stool and slowly walks in a semi-circle. Katherine and Caitlin click their heels against the partition and jiggle up & down.

TABLEAU 5 – a blindfolded blonde-haired girl is walking down the staircase. She guides herself with the bannister.

As Stephanie moves from the wall toward Temple, each stretch their arms out in front of themselves.

Deep Voice: `May-be, may-be, you'd better not go there.`

Temple and Stephanie touch hands then turn toward the audience.

Bulb flash.

33:02 The revolving lights of the clocktower are turned on.
Stephanie removes her blindfold & Temple sits back down on the stool.

Sound cue: *idea bell.*

TABLEAU 5 – WOMAN in blindfold: "If I were to postulate ..."

33:13 **TABLEAU 5 – left-wipe to a tilted version of the same scene.**

Temple leans further back as Ben stands over her. Stephanie runs over and places her hands on the side of Temple's head.

Sound cue: *ringing phone, eerie noise.*

High-pitched Voice: `Now, now, right now.`

Sound cue: *haunting whisper.*

Voice: `Five, three, and two.`

33:33

High-pitched Voice: Ri, di di di di di di di de dooo; twee, ri di di di di di di do daaa.

Female Voice: Chan-te a-vec moi.

TABLEAU 5 – WOMAN on screen in blindfold: "If I were to postulate time passing –"

33:40 **TABLEAU 5** – left-wipe to WOMAN in blindfold: "If you were to postulate time passing –"

Kathleen and Caitlin rise from the partition, each holding a sword in the air as they face the stage-right wall.

High-pitched Voice: Ri, di di di di di di di de dooo; twee, ri di di di di di di do daaa.

Sound cue: *shattering glass, scraping noise.*

High-pitched Voice: Ri, di di di di di di di de dooo; twee, ri di di di di di di do daaa.

33:54 Ben wheels the clocktower to stage left.
Kathleen and Caitlin run off stage.

Deep Voice: Look.

Voice: Va-voom. Va-voom.

Voice track: Ff-fleeeewdkey, bi, bi, bi, bi, beep; o-ca, o-ca, o-ca, o-ca.

Deep Voice: Look.

Voice track: `Ff-fleeeewdkey, bi, bi, bi, bi, beep; o-ca, o-ca, o-ca, o-ca.`

Temple rises from the stool. Katherine takes it and walks off stage.

Deep Voice: `Look.`

TABLEAU 5 – WOMAN: "Suppose I were to postulate, time passing means things are always under control. How would you deal with that?"

Screen flare.

TEMPLE (blindfolded): Fly a-way giant mys-tic don-key peo-ple.

Sound cue: *shattering glass, scraping noise.*

Temple walks toward the partitions at stage right; Ben approaches her, gently places his hands on her shoulders, then draws her back to center stage.

Deep Voice: `Say it a-gain and a-gain. Say it a-gain and a-gain. Please let me in.`

Screen flare.

TABLEAU 5 – WOMAN: "Suppose I were to postulate: time passing means that things are always under control. How would you deal with that?"

Ben releases Temple's hands, then backs away from her and crouching, swiftly rolls his hands over one another in a backwards circle. Caitlin approaches Temple and removes her blindfold, then wraps it around the back of her neck and walks stage right while leaning backwards.

Temple smacks Ben on the back; as she runs away, he chases her while making the same hand motions.

Sound cue: *eerie noise, shattering glass.*

34:44 Screen flares out.

British Female Voice: Seen and not heard. Seen and not heard.

RULES FOR BEGINNERS?

Deep Voice: Re-mem-ber. Mi-stakes, mi-stakes have been made.

Ben stands center stage and continuously smacks his fists against his head.

Deep Voice: Don't look. No mi-stake. [Sound cue: *computer blip.*] Those pre-disposed to hap-pi-ness, see (Hap-pi-ness) no-thing, hear no-thing.

35:08 **TABLEAU 5** – a woman in a black dress stands on the staircase while holding a white blindfold. She stares backwards toward a blindfolded woman in a black dress.

PRIVATE

Ben holds a stick with a lettered cube on each end toward the audience, then toward the upstage screen. Caitlin brings a sheet of newspaper to Temple; she quickly crumples it. Katherine brings her a sheet of newspaper, which she also quickly crumples into a ball and throws on the ground. Katherine picks up the newspaper balls and walks off stage. Temple takes the stick from Ben & places it on the upstage screen ledge.

Deep Voice: May-be, may-be, you'd better not go there.

Sound cue: *eerie noise, scraping noise.*

35:17

PRIVATE

PRIVATE PERFORMANCE

Temple opens the window at the bottom of the upstage screen while Ben opens the window on the stage-left screen. Bright light streams out of each window.

Music cue: *modernist violin.*

Sound cue: *scraping noise.*

35:36 **TABLEAU 5** – wipe-tilt to same scene.

Sound cue: *scraping noise; humming, which increases in volume.*

35:46 **TABLEAU 6** – wipe to a man sitting in a chair and two blind-folded women on a couch. WOMAN: "If you were to postulate time passing means things are always under control. I would have to deal with that."

Screen flare.

36:03

BACKWARDS / UNDER CONTROL

Sound cue: *humming noise stops.*

Screen panel lights flare off. Ben and Temple close the windows.

TABLEAU 6 – woman in red dress enters and bends down; she grabs a piece of newspaper, crumples it.

36:21

THAT INEVITABLE DONKEY

Music cue: *gentle melodic tune with vocal in French.*

TABLEAU 6 – WOMAN: "Suppose I were to postulate, an opinion must always be an [sound cue: *chime*] internal misunderstanding. How would you deal with that?"

Bulb flash; white flare washes out the screens.

Ben takes a sword from Temple and places it back in the partition. Katherine and Caitlin enter with the donkey billboard from stage left; they are wearing sunglasses and pointed white caps with tassels. Stephanie also enters wearing sunglasses with dark black round lenses and a pointed white cap with a tassel, retrieves a sword from the stage-right wall, then places it in the partition.

36:46

'INEVITABLE' SHORT CIRCUIT?

Stephanie & Ben rock back and forth while straddling the partition. Katherine and Caitlin carry the stuffed donkey across the stage as Temple stares at the upstage screen.

Sound cue: *computer blip, eerie noise.*

Bulb flash.

37:06 Bulb flash.

Music cue: *modernist piano.*

TABLEAU 6 – WOMAN: "Suppose I were to postulate, an opinion must always be an internal misunderstanding. How would you deal with that?"

Sound cue: *ringing phone.*

Deep Voice: `Once on-ly.`

Stephanie and Ben rock back and forth on the partition.

Sound cue: *clicking noise.*

Temple takes the stuffed donkey from Katherine and Caitlin and places it on one of the black partitions, then gently bangs it against the pole six times [sound cue: *donkey hee-haw (6x)*].

37:36 Temple throws the stuffed donkey on the ground. Stephanie and Ben rock back and forth while straddling the partition.

Sound cue: *eerie noise, clicking noise.*

TABLEAU 6 – WOMAN: "If you were to postulate, an opinion must be an internal misunderstanding, I would have to deal with that."

Katherine and Caitlin pick up the stuffed donkey then drop it behind the donkey billboard.

KATHERINE / CAITLIN (whispering in falsetto in unison): Fly, fly, fly, mystic donkey, fly, fly – ooooooooooo.

Temple blindfolds herself, then walks to the stage-left screen and opens the panel. Light streams out of it. She walks to the upstage screen and opens the panel. Light also streams out as the light bulbs on the upstage screen ledge flare on.

38:18 **TABLEAU 6 – girl in red dress crosses from the right to the left of the screen.**

Temple moves to center stage and removes her blindfold. The triple-paneled billboard is unfolded to display three donkeys. Ben and Stephanie take a sword and twist it against the donkey billboard as Katherine & Caitlin close the screen panels, then walk to center stage with Stephanie. While facing the audience, they lift their arms and point at the stage-left screen.

Bulb flash.

38:47

Deep Voice: `Im-pos-si-ble.`

TEMPLE: 5, 3, and 2.

Katherine, Caitlin, & Stephanie retrieve the stuffed donkey, lift it into the air, then carry it off stage.

39:13 Temple removes a pillow from under the stage-left screen then moves to center stage and holds it against her chest. SHE stares at the audience, says "1, 2," then turns back toward the stage-left screen.

Deep Voice: `In-ev-i-ta-ble be-hav-ior.`

TABLEAU 6 – girl in red dress walks from left to right.

Sound cue: *alarm.*

Voice (stridently): `No, no, no, you have to go back and do it again. This is not the way to do it. Believe me. This is not the way to do it. Go back! Go back!`

Music cue: *fast harpsichord.*

Voice: `Ex-per-ience. Ex-per-ience.`

39:41 **TABLEAU 6 – wipe from left to right to man in suit with yellow tie sitting in chair.**

Deep Voice: `Don-key.`

Screen flare.

Temple places the pillow over her head then runs into the stage-left wall.

All of the actors moan.

Music cue: *fast harpsichord continues, increasing in volume.*

Voice: `Va-voom. Va-voom.`

Sound cue: *shattering glass.*

39:48 **TABLEAU 7** – wipe to a large room with a woman on all fours in a blindfold; another woman sits on top of her. The man in the chair from the previous scene is visible in the background.

Ben enters wearing a white pointed hat with a red cape. He holds two star-crowned scepters above his head and walks in a circle as Katherine, Stephanie, and Caitlin roll one of the Giant Eyeballs to center stage, then hold a red & black checkerboard with a gold frame above the object. Ben swings the scepter toward the checkerboard but does not hit it, then [sound cue: *smashing glass*] monotonously drums against it.

Music cue: *solo opera voice commences as the harpsichord track fades out.*

40:16 **TABLEAU 7** – a woman in a grey dress is sitting on top of a woman in a black dress squatting on all fours.

PRIVATE PERFORMANCE

Voice: a professor lecturing in German on Beethoven.

Sound cue: *ringing phone.*

Ben continues monotonously drumming the checkerboard.

TABLEAU 7 – a woman enters the foreground, filling the right side of the screen, then another woman enters immediately after her.

Ben stops drumming.

Music cue: *solo baritone.*

40:46 **TABLEAU 7** — a woman in a grey dress is sitting on top of a woman in a black dress squatting on all fours.

Deep Voice: `A weight pul-ling one to the cen-ter of things.`

TEMPLE: Five, three, and two.

40:55

THAT INEVITABLE DONKEY

Sound cue: *computer blip.*

Bulb flash.

Music cue: *discordant violin.*

Deep Voice: `As a re-min-der.`

TABLEAU 7 — Blindfolded WOMAN: "Suppose I were to postulate — there must be something wrong with a face that is always the same face. How would you deal with that?"

Sound cue: *alarm bell (3x).*

Ben monotonously drums against the checkerboard.

Bulb flash (3x).

Stephanie enters with a toy house and places it on the ground.

41:28 **TABLEAU 7 — wipe to same scene.**

Sound cue: *alarm bell (2x).*

Stephanie lifts the toy house into the air. Temple sticks her hand inside the window of the top floor. She removes a doll, holds it between her fingers, then moves to the checkerboard and spins the doll between her hands.

Voice: `Ff-fleeeewdkey, bi, bi, bi, bi, beep; o-ca, o-ca, o-ca, o-ca.`

Music cue: *modernist piano.*

Sound cue: *alarm bell.*

Voice: `Ri, di di di di di di di de dooo; twee, ri di di di di di di do daaa.`

Caitlin removes the checkerboard from above the Eye. Katherine rolls the Eye off stage. Stephanie kneels before the stage-left screen while Ben drags another object off stage. Caitlin places the checkerboard on the ground and Temple rests the toy house on top of it.

TABLEAU 7 — two women enter the foreground. Another woman enters in the background.

Sound cue: *haunting whisper.*

Music cue: *modernist violin.*

TEMPLE: Five, three, and two.

Deep Voice: `Fol-ded, self-fol-ded (fol-ded).`

Katherine, Ben, and Stephanie enter and crouch on all fours in a line, one behind the other, facing stage left. Temple mounts Ben and Caitlin mounts Stephanie.

42:31

Sound cue: *scraping noise.*

TABLEAU 7 – the women in the foreground and background exit. GIRL: "Suppose I were to postulate – there must be something wrong with a face that is always the same face. How would you deal with that?"

Deep Voice: 1, 2, 3, 4, 5.

Temple dismounts Ben then kneels before the toy house and stares into the second story window.

Music cue: *string plucks, modernist piano.*

Caitlin dismounts Stephanie and turns to face the upstage screen. Katherine, Ben, Temple, and Caitlin walk off stage.

43:12

Music cue: *modernist piano.*

TABLEAU 7 – GIRL: "Suppose I were to postulate – there must be something wrong with a face that is always the same face. How would you deal with that?"

Deep Voice (overlapping): 1, 2, 3, 4, 5.

Katherine, Stephanie, and Caitlin enter with a red cushioned chair.

Music cue: *accordion track from Mihály Vig's score to Béla Tarr's* Werckmeister Harmóniák.

Deep Voice: I'm happy to tell you (1, 2, 3, 4, 5) – Those pre-disposed to hap-pi-ness –

Sound cue: *shattering glass, Chinese gong.*

Bulb flash.

Ben takes a stuffed donkey and places it against the stage-right wall.

TABLEAU 7 – woman riding the other woman removes her blindfold then exits.

43:42

ACCURATE MENTAL COPIES ?

Bulb flash.

Deep Voice: See nothing, Hear nothing. Look. (Ac-cur-rate.)

Voice: Ff-fleeeewdkey, bi, bi, bi, bi, beep; o-ca, o-ca, o-ca, o-ca.

TABLEAU 7 – woman returns and puts the blindfold on the woman in the red dress, who is sitting on a couch behind the 'donkey woman.'

Ben lifts a stuffed donkey off the ground and throws it between the black partitions.

Temple lifts the toy house into the air and carries it off stage.

43:52

Deep Voice: `Pri-vate (Pri-vate) per-for-mance.`

Sound cue: *chime.*

Screen flare.

Ben pretends kicking the stuffed donkey then returns to his previous position and places his hands on his hips and stares into the audience.

TABLEAU 7 – wipe to **WOMAN**: "If I were to postulate – there must be something wrong with a face that's always the same face ..."

44:21 **TABLEAU 7** – wipe to **WOMAN**: "I would have to deal, deal with that."

Sound cue: *computer blip; wood block.*

Ben, Katherine, and Stephanie raise the donkey billboard at an angle across the front of the upstage screen.

Sound cue: *alarm bell (3x).*

Deep Voice: `Mi-stakes have been made. Don't look. No mi-stake.`

Screen flare. Image washes out.

Music cue: Werckmeister Harmóniák *accordion track returns.*

Caitlin stands back and points at the donkey billboard as she faces the audience.

Bulb flash.

Ben, Katherine, and Stephanie lower the billboard to the ground. Caitlin retrieves a sledgehammer from under the stage-left wall and brings it to Ben, who places it on the ground.

45:18 Screen flare + ceiling light flare (3x).

Caitlin picks up the sledgehammer and carries it across stage. She hands it to Ben, who holds it against his chest then places it on the checkerboard. Caitlin retrieves it and walks to center stage, facing the upstage screen.

45:26 **TABLEAU 8** – left-wipe to crawl-dance: in a large room, a blindfolded woman in a red dress stands at the edge of the frame; in front of her kneels a group of men. Light streams into the room through two windows.

Bulb flash.

Stephanie pulls the red cushioned chair back toward the stage-left screen. TEMPLE runs into the same wall while holding a pillow over her head and shouting: "Ooooooooo."

Sound cue: *shattering glass.*

Music cue: Werckmeister Harmóniák *accordion track increases in volume, then decreases.*

Ben crawls along the ground, then collapses and places his feet on the black piping. Stephanie lifts the giant eyeball and places it between two partitions. Katherine holds the checkerboard over the Eyeball. Caitlin swings the sledgehammer over it.

46:02 **TABLEAU 8 — wipe to same scene.**

Katherine removes the checkerboard. Stephanie takes the Eyeball and places it on the ground where the checkerboard previously was. Caitlin carries the sledgehammer & stands behind Temple, then rests it on top of the chair.

Music cue: *accordion track increases in volume, then stops.*

Stephanie rests her head against the Eyeball. Katherine lies next to her and places her finger over her lips. Temple lifts a white cloth from the ground, places it on the seat, then sits on it and slowly wiggles her ass over the cloth as Caitlin walks in front of Stephanie & Katherine, stares at them, then swings herself over the partition to lay next to Katherine.

Voice (stridently): No, no, no, no. You have to go back and do it again. That is not the way to do it. Believe me. This is not the way to do it. Go back! Go back!

Sound cue: *war siren.*

Bulb flash.

Sound cue: *haunting whisper.*

Deep Voice: Once on-ly.

Screen flare. Image washes out.

Temple walks toward Ben as if to touch him, then retreats to the chair, removes the white cloth, places it over Ben's face.

Deep Voice: Fol-ded, self-fol-ded (fol-ded).

Sound cue: *plastic drum.*

46:55

(HAPPINESS)

TABLEAU 8 – wipe to same scene from a different angle but with just the people on the floor.

Bulb flash (2x).

Temple gently lowers a sledgehammer onto the Giant Eyeball as if to strike it, then lifts the sledgehammer, rests it on her shoulder, stares at the audience.

47:13

PROBLEM / NO PROBLEM

Bulb flash.

47:21 **TABLEAU 8** – the woman in the red dress enters and shimmies and jiggles before the men while holding her arms aloft, then walks away.

Music cue: *solo clarinet.*

Sound cue: *wood block clack.*

(HAPPINESS)

Deep Voice: `It would be fine in-deed [sound cue:` *shattering glass* `] (Per-fect) if there were rules for beginners.`

Music cue: *modernist piano, violin.*

TABLEAU 8 – woman runs back into the group and shimmies & jiggles.

Stephanie lifts the Eyeball into the air with both of her hands. Ben rises and stares at the object, then takes it from her as Temple walks to stage left and covers her right eye with her hand, then moves it down along her chest and turns to face the upstage screen.

Ben carries the Eyeball to the upstage screen & holds it against the center of the screen.

Screen flare; bulb flash (4x).

48:00 Bulb flash (2x).

Ben removes the Giant Eyeball from the screen and faces the audience while holding the object above his head.

Deep Voice: `I'm hap-py to tell you, somebody else picks up the ball and runs with it and does other, hard im-pos-si-ble things.`

Voice (overlapping with Deep Voice): `Ri, di di di di di di di de dooo; twee, ri di di di di di di do daaa.`

Music cue: *modernist clarinet & violin.*

Caitlin takes the Eyeball away from Ben and carries it stage right, then holds it in front of a vertical black pole, its iris facing the audience.

Voice: Ri, di di di di di di di de dooo; twee, ri di di di di di di do daaa.

48:42 Stephanie drags the ceremonial chair to stage right, behind the partitions. Temple carries a stuffed donkey to center stage then hands it to Stephanie, who carries it to the partition.

TABLEAU 8 — wipe into an earlier scene and then zoom to men crawling on the floor.

(NO PROBLEM)

Bulb flash (2x).

Sound cue: *eerie noises.*

48:50

THE REAL DONKEY THE INEVITABLE DONKEY. THAT INEVITABLE DONKEY DID NOT MOVE. THAT BEAST OF THE INEVITABLE REAL BURDEN.

Stephanie holds one stuffed donkey up to a stage-right window out of which light streams. Katherine holds another stuffed donkey against it, its nose pressed into the ass of the other donkey.

48:52 **TABLEAU 8** – wipe to the same scene.

Bulb flash (2x).

Ben takes one donkey from Katherine and carries it upside down to center stage then drops it on the ground. Caitlin places the Giant Eyeball on the ground. Stephanie crouches behind her. Katherine throws the other donkey behind the black partition.

TABLEAU 8 – woman in red dress enters and shimmies & jiggles. Freeze frame.

Music cue: *strange, haunting music.*

49:34 **TABLEAU 8** – wipe to same scene. Screen flare. Image washes out.

Music cue: *fast harpsichord.*

Deep Voice: `Per-fect.`

Ben stares at the upstage screen.

TABLEAU 8 – woman in red dress enters and shimmies & jiggles. Freeze frame.

Deep Voice: `Per-fect.`

TABLEAU 8 – woman in red dress enters and dances again. Freeze frame.

50:13

Sound cue: *alarm bell (2x).*

Deep Voice: `Sup-pose. Sup-pose I were to pos-tu-late.`

TABLEAU 8 – WOMAN: "Suppose I were to postulate. I had totally forgotten that every opportunity produces mental confusion."

Voice: `Ri, di di di di di di di de dooo; twee, ri di di di di di di do daaa.`

Screen flare.

Voice #2 (to repeating computer ding): `Coo, coo (2X).`

Deep Voice: `May-be, may-be, you'd better not go there.`

Voice #2 (to repeating computer ding): `Coo, coo (2X).`

Music cue: *brief angular piano track.*

Temple walks to center stage, stretches her arms out in front of her, then holds her hands together and points at the audience.

50:48 TEMPLE: Don-key, don-key.

TABLEAU 8 – woman with red dress enters and shimmies & jiggles then exits. Freeze frame.

Deep Voice: `Don-key.`

TEMPLE: You and me.

Music cue: *modernist piano.*

51:01

THE SOLID PART OF EXISTENCE

TEMPLE (as she turns and faces the stage-left screen): One is prisoner. [Kicks her right leg three times] Donkey, don-key, you and me.

Bulb flash, screen flare.

51:14

THE REAL DONKEY

Bulb flash, screen flare.

TEMPLE (in sing-song voice): One is prisoner, one is free. Pray for me, pray for me.

TABLEAU 8 – woman in red dress enters and shimmies & jiggles.

Sound cue: *thumping drum (3x).*

Ben, Katherine, Caitlin, and Stephanie each kick one leg into the air six times [sound cue: *kick drum (6x)*].

TEMPLE: Don-key, don-key, you and me.

Deep Voice: Don-key.

Sound cue: *alarm bell; soft gong.*

TEMPLE (in sing-song voice): One is prisoner, one is free. [Sound cue: `elephant roar (3X).`] Pray for me, pray for me.

`51:50`

British Female Voice: `Seen and not heard. Seen and not heard.`

Ben walks to center stage with a toy gun at his side and stares into the audience.

BEN: Don-key, don-key, you and me.

Katherine, Stephanie, and Caitlin each blindfold themselves then step forward carrying one lettered cube in each hand. They drop the cubes.

BEN: One is prisoner, one is free.

KATHERINE and CAITLIN scream softly in falsetto, their voices rising in crescendo and falling. Ben retrieves two of the cubes, carries them to Temple, then places them in her hands.

TEMPLE: Now I know my ABCs.

Temple drops the cubes.

`52:24` **TABLEAU 9 – wipe to a woman in a burgundy dress lying on the ground held by three other people.**

TEMPLE: Don't hit me; don't punish me. ABC.

Voice: `Ex-per-ience. Ex-per-ience.`

Sound cue: *chime.*

TEMPLE (elongating each letter): A—, B—, C—.

Music cue: *modernist piano, violin.*

Ben picks up the cubes again and drops them on the ground like dice.

Deep Voice: `In-ev-i-ta-ble be-hav-ior.`

Caitlin wheels the ceremonial chair back to center stage.

Katherine, Stephanie, and Temple, who are kneeling on the ground before the donkey billboard, all raise their arms in unison as if performing a benediction.

53:03 **TABLEAU 9 – left-wipe to same scene.**

Music cue: *modernist piano, violin continues.*

53:08

UNDER CONTROL / BACKWARDS ?

Light flare.

Music cue: *modernist piano, violin increasing in volume.*

TABLEAU 9 – WOMAN: "If I were to propose feelings for other people like glass, touchable, but not seen – how would you deal with that?"

Screen flare.

Ben leans over the chair and retrieves a rounded mirror-shaped object with a red and white bull's-eye. He bends over the chair and rubs the object against his ass in a counterclockwise motion then holds it before himself and stares into it.

Deep Voice: In-ev-i-ta-ble. In-ev-i-ta-ble.

BEN (pointing at the object): A—, B—, C—.

Bulb flash.

53:48

Deep Voice (with a strong emphasis on each syllable): They do it on a don-key.

Bulb flash; screen flare.

BEN (in slow ecstatic drawl): AA—, BB—, CC—.

STEPHANIE, TEMPLE, CAITLIN, & KATHERINE (barking and humping in unison while straddling the black partitions): O, o, o, o, o, o, o, o.

BEN (in slow ecstatic drawl): AA—, BB—, CC—.

Deep Voice (with a strong emphasis on each syllable): They do it in a hole in the wall. [Sound cue: *donkey squeal.*] They do it where they find me hi-ding. [Sound cue: *donkey hee-haw (3x)*.] The (don-key) best of all; BUT best of all, they are go-ing to do it; they are go-ing to do it. The sun is shi-ning. [Sound cue: *soft gong.*] (Hap-pi-ness.) But who can do it?

54:59

SUPPOSE?

The actresses each begin writing on the stage-right wall in white chalk.

TABLEAU 9 — a woman runs across the screen.

Deep Voice: `They do not do it. Why should they do it? A lifetime is an accurate –. 3, 4, 5. 1, 2, 3, 4, 5.`

Ben walks to the upstage screen and stares at it.

55:27 Bulb flash.

Sound cue: *chime, eerie humming.*

TABLEAU 9 — WOMAN: "If I were to propose, feelings for other people like glass, touchable ... but not seen. I would have to deal with that."

Bulb flash.

BEN (howls with a strong emphasis on each syllable): I [sound cue: *glass smashing*] do it on the don-key.

FEMALE ACTORS IN UNISON: One!

Sound cue: *clicking, eerie humming.*

BEN (with a strong emphasis on each syllable): I do it where they find me hi-ding.

Deep Voice: `Well.`

FEMALE ACTORS IN UNISON: Two!

TABLEAU 9 — WOMAN: "If I were to propose, feelings for other people like glass, touchable ... but not seen — how would you deal with that?"

56:16

A 'REMINDER' ONLY ?

TABLEAU 9 – WOMAN: "If I were to propose, feelings for other people like glass, touchable ... but not seen – how would you deal with that?"

Bulb flash.

Deep Voice: They do it on a don-key.

BEN (singing with a strong emphasis on each syllable): They do it in a hole in the wall.

Deep Voice: They do it in a hole in the wall.

Temple places the Giant Eyeball on top of the red cushioned chair, the iris facing the audience, while Caitlin picks up a stuffed donkey and embraces it as she leans against a stage-right partition.

56:43 **TABLEAU 10** – flare and wipe to a group of woman clad in black standing in a line and stretching into the distance. They hold their hands together in prayer.

Screen flare.

Music cue: *strange, haunting music.*

SUPPOSE

Deep Voice (fading in and out): `They do it where they find me hi-ding. BUT best of all; but best of all, they are going to do it. Well. They are going to do it.`

Ben wheels the clocktower to center stage. While facing the audience, Temple places her hand over the bull's-eye on the billboard donkey's ass. Stephanie takes a white cloth and rubs the tower as if cleaning it.

57:10 **TABLEAU 10 – WOMAN:** "Suppose I were to postulate, disappearing into the before I was born and disappearing into the after I am dead – how would you deal with that?"

Screen flare.

Sound cue: *ringing phone, war siren (3x).*

Music cue: *modernist piano & violin.*

Deep Voice: `Pri-vate re-min-der.`

TABLEAU 10 – the women all stare into the camera and remain still.

Stephanie returns to rubbing the tower. Temple, who is sitting in the red cushioned chair, reaches out and holds her hand over the iris of the Giant Eyeball.

Music cue: *strange, haunting music.*

Voice (stridently): `No, no, no, no. You have to go back and do it again. This is not the way to do it. Believe me. This is not the way to do it. Go back! Go back!`

Sound cue: *donkey hee-haw (3x).*

57:51 **TABLEAU 10** — WOMAN: "Suppose I were to postulate, disappearing into the before I was born and disappearing into the after I am dead — how would you deal with that?"

Sound cue: *buzzing.*

Music cue: *strange, haunting music continues.*

Deep Voice (overlapping with Music cue): `Once on-ly.`

STEPHANIE (shouting, while continuing to rub the tower clean): One, two – right – !

Deep Voice: `Pri-vate. Strangers are not permitted to view this pri-vate, per-for-mance.`

Ben, Katherine, and Caitlin enter with red-and-grey striped cellos & stand just left of center stage, resting their hands and head on the peg box of the cello.

58:23

PRIVATE

Screen flare.

Sound cue: *war siren, shattering glass.*

Deep Voice: `When the men-tal fin-gers touch the sur-face of things – look (Im-pos-si-ble). Look. 3, 4, 5.`

TABLEAU 10 — wipe to same scene.

Female Voice: ethereal singing.

High-pitched Voice: Now, now, right now.

Sound cue: *chime.*

Deep Voice: Once on-ly. 1, 2, 3, 4. 5. Pri-vate.

Temple slowly walks toward Ben, then kneels down behind the plexiglass partition, retrieves an object, then rises and turns toward the stage-left screen.

59:30 **TABLEAU 9**

NO OTHER WORLD IS REAL

Screen flare.

Deep Voice: Re-mind-er.

Sound cue: *ringing phone (4x).*

Female Voice: ethereal singing continues.

Ben, Katherine, and Caitlin sit and hold their cellos with one hand while they hold their right hands against their heads. Stephanie runs out with a stuffed donkey all the way up to Ben, then backs up and crouches with the donkey before the Giant Eyeball.

Sound cue: *shattering glass.*

Deep Voice: One, two, three, four, five.

1:00:20 **TABLEAU 9**

SEEN AND NOT HEARD?

Bulb flash.

Music cue: *haunting trumpet & vocal.*

Bulb flash.

1:00:35 **TABLEAU 9**

A 'REMINDER' ONLY?

Bulb flash.

Deep Voice: That beast of the in-evi-ta-ble (In-ev-i-ta-ble).

Sound cue: *war siren, ringing phone.*

BEN (lifting his head and elongating each letter and word): Ooooooooo, oooooooo, oooooooo, but they do it on the don-key.

Deep Voice: `Well. Well.`

Sound cue: *donkey hee-haw (5x); war siren.*

TEMPLE: Fly a-way, old fash-ioned, worn-out don-key. Fly a-way, don-key, don-key.

Voice: `Ex-per-ience. Ex-per-ience.`

`Ba, ba, ba, ba, ba, ba, baaaaa, noooooooon, noooooon, ah-na kaaan, zooooo, yidi yidi yidi hoooooo, noooooon, zooooon, ti, nooooon, zooooon, dah doo, zoodah, zidi dah doont.`

`Ex-per-ience. Ex-per-ience.`

Music cue: *haunting double trumpet.*

Katherine, Ben, and Caitlin take their cellos and each straddle one of the black partitions as they slide the stand of their cellos into a hole at the top of each partition.

Temple blindfolds herself, then grasps the peg box of Caitlin's cello then lets it go.

1:02:02 **TABLEAU 9 — the woman wraps a blindfold on her head.**

Temple walks to the stage-right window and stares into the light. Ben, Caitlin, and Katherine all turn back to stare at her.

Voice (at low volume, then increasing): `a professor lecturing in German on Beethoven.`

Katherine, Ben, & Caitlin each turn back, then lean forward and tear a thin paper scroll from out of the body of their cellos and begin pulling it further out. Simultaneously, Temple is pulling a similar but wider scroll from out of the window into which she is staring.

Sound cue: *swooshing computer sound (3x); smashing glass.*

All the actors stop and stare at each scroll, curiously examining them.

Sound cue: *shattering glass.*

1:02:49 **TABLEAU 10** – Woman: "Suppose I were to postulate, disappearing into the before I was born and disappearing into the after I am dead – how would you deal with that?"

Deep Voice: `Sup-pose (Nor-mal). Sup-pose.`

Voice (increasing in volume): `a professor lecturing in German on Beethoven continues.`

TABLEAU 10 – WOMAN: "Suppose I were to postulate, disappearing into the before I was born and disappearing into the after I am dead – how would you deal with that?"

Katherine, Ben, & Caitlin slowly pull more and more of the scroll out of the body of their respective cellos while Stephanie kneels on the ground before them as if trying to decipher the script, which is covered in Hebrew letters.

Katherine, Ben, and Caitlin then rest their heads against the peg boxes of their respective cellos as Temple continues trying to decipher the script on her scroll.

1:03:00

Music cue: *haunting double trumpet plays out.*

Voice (slowly fades out): a professor lecturing on Beethoven.

1:04:03 **FADE TO BLACK**

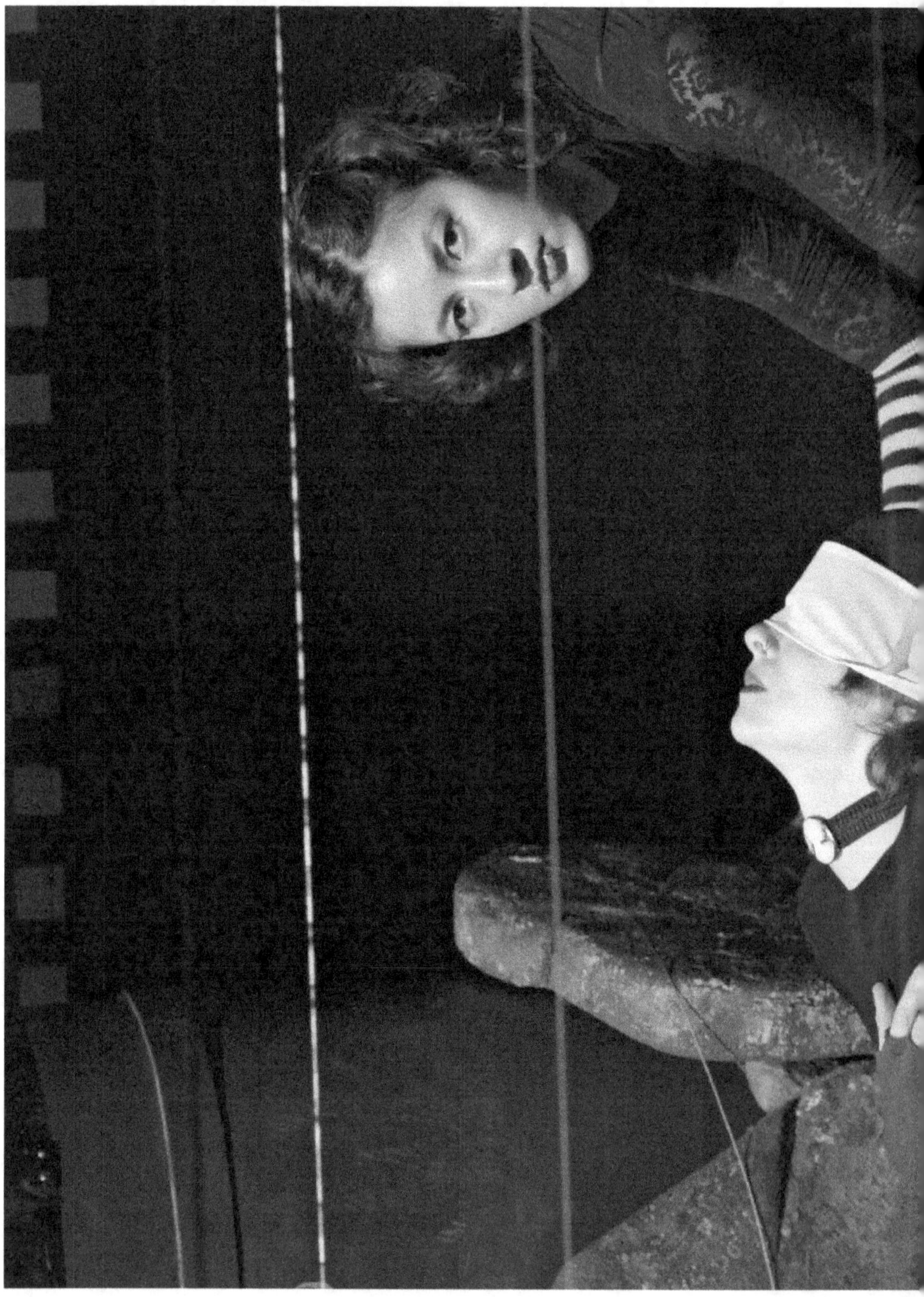

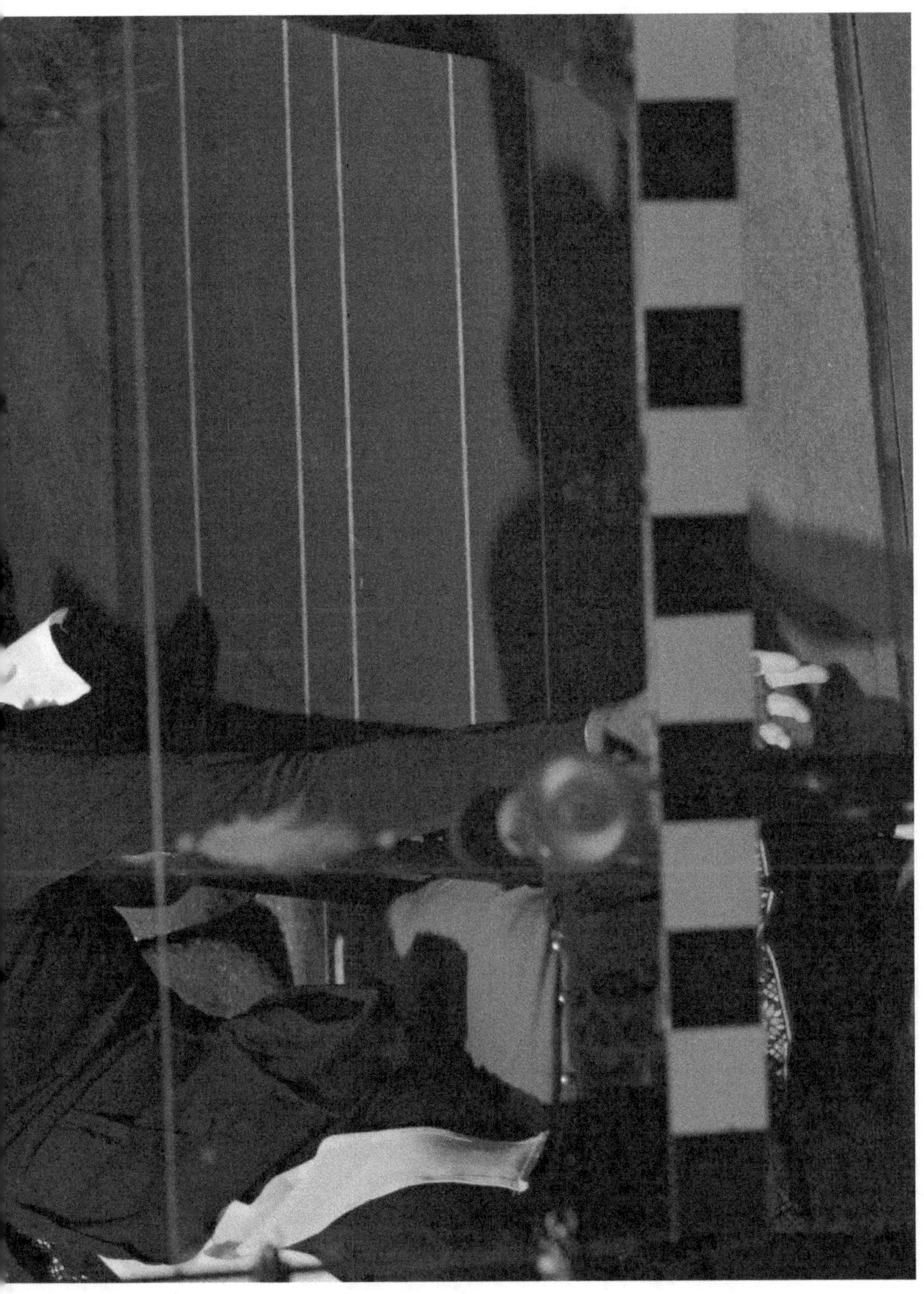

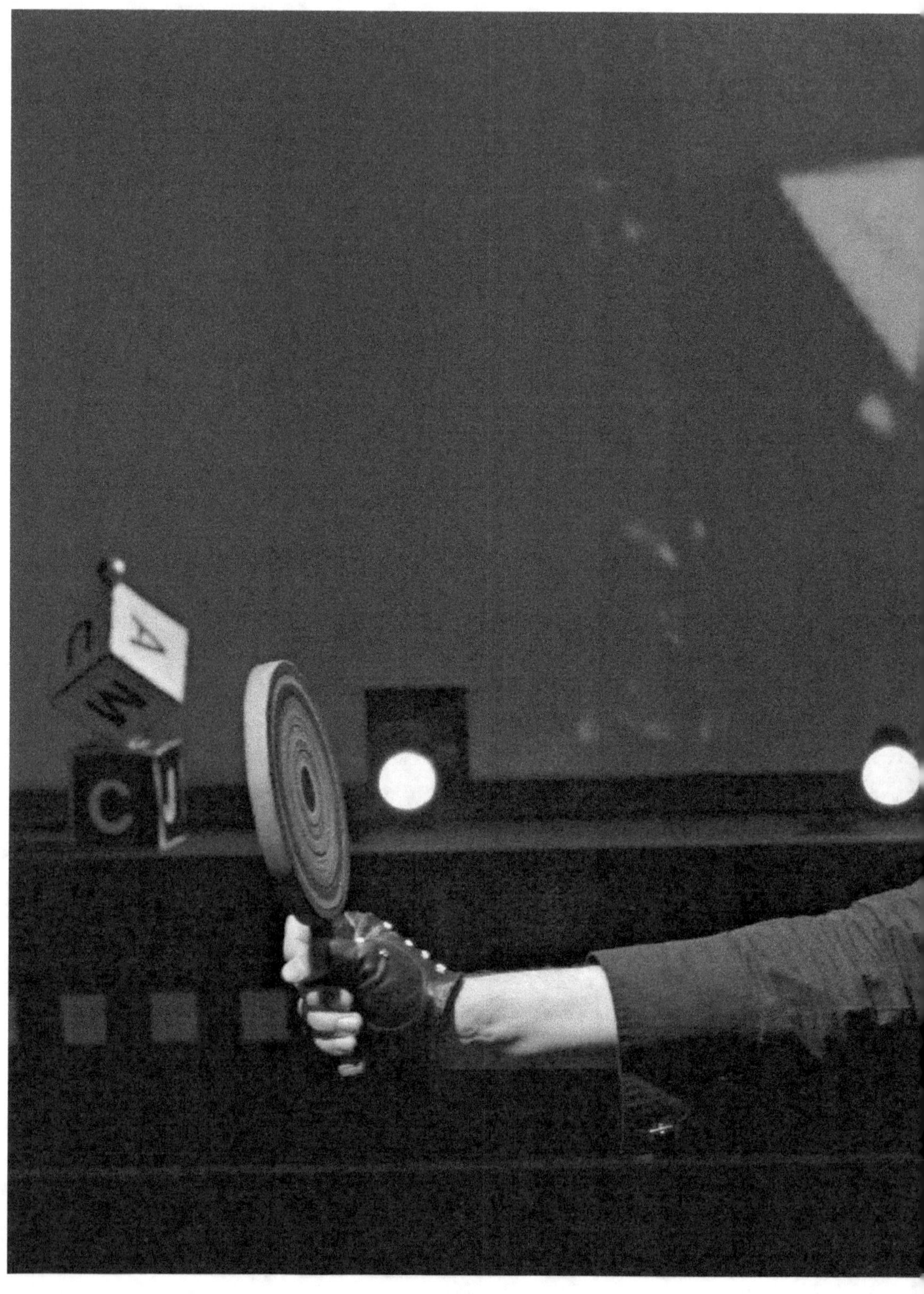

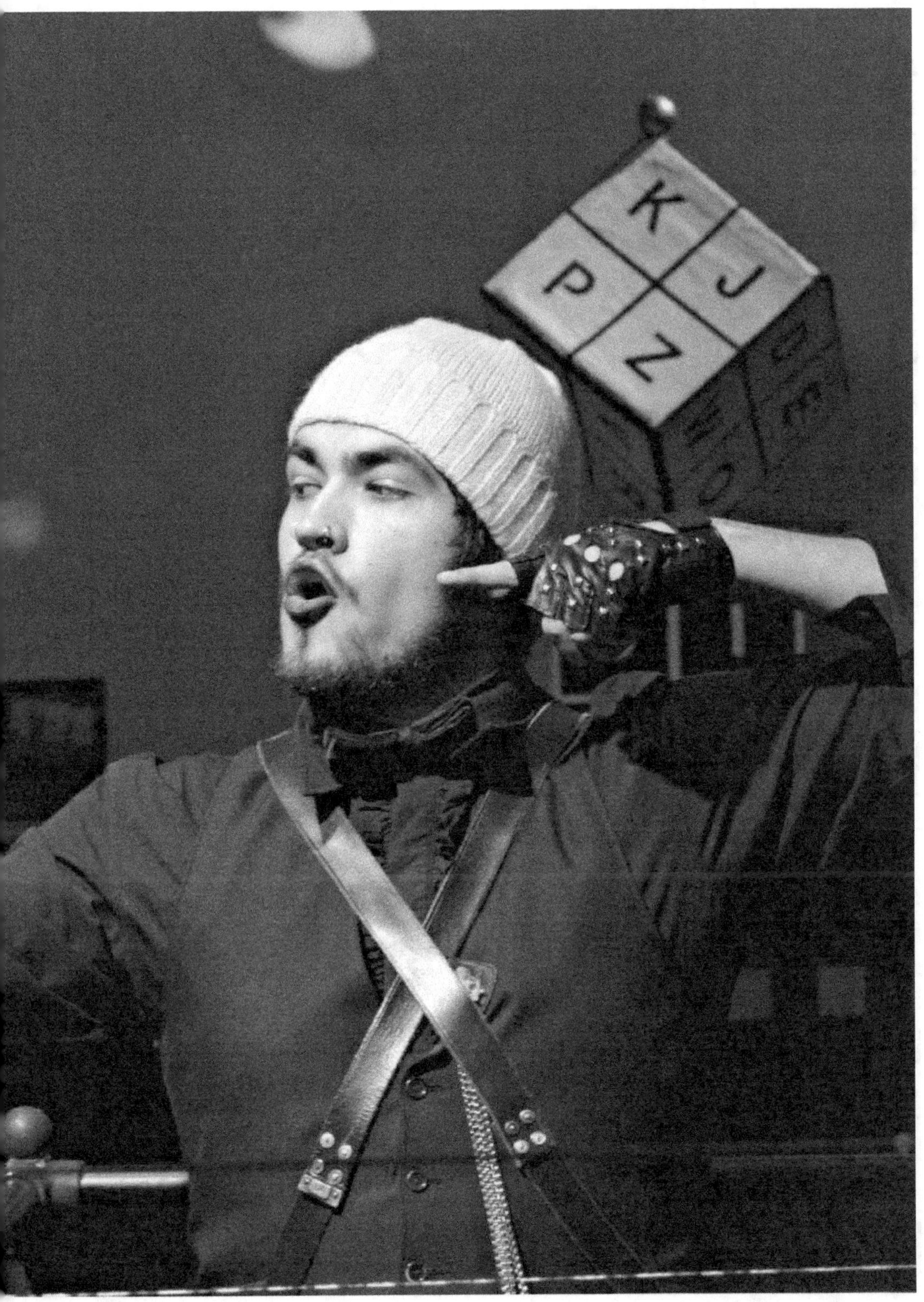
K
P
J
Z

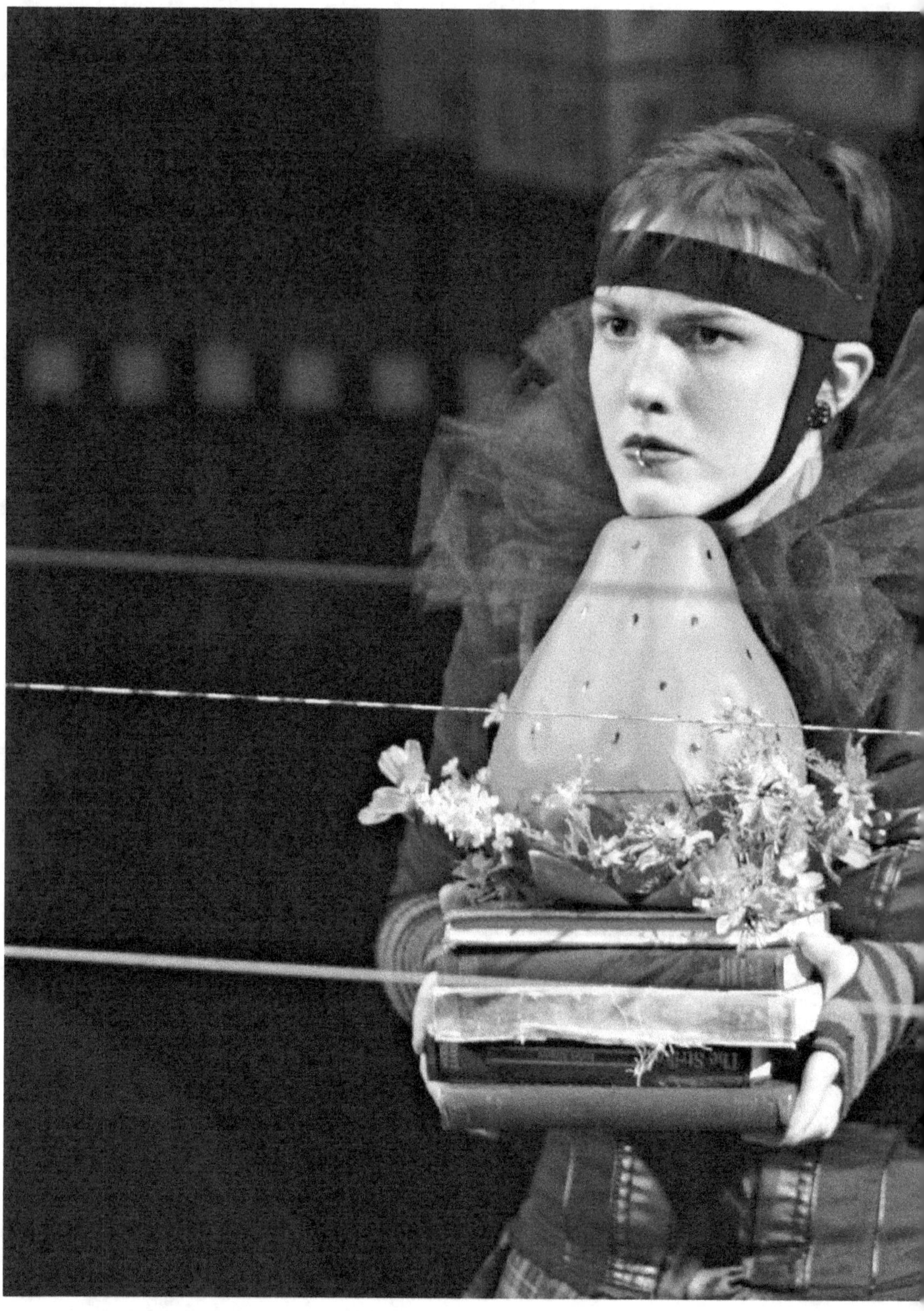

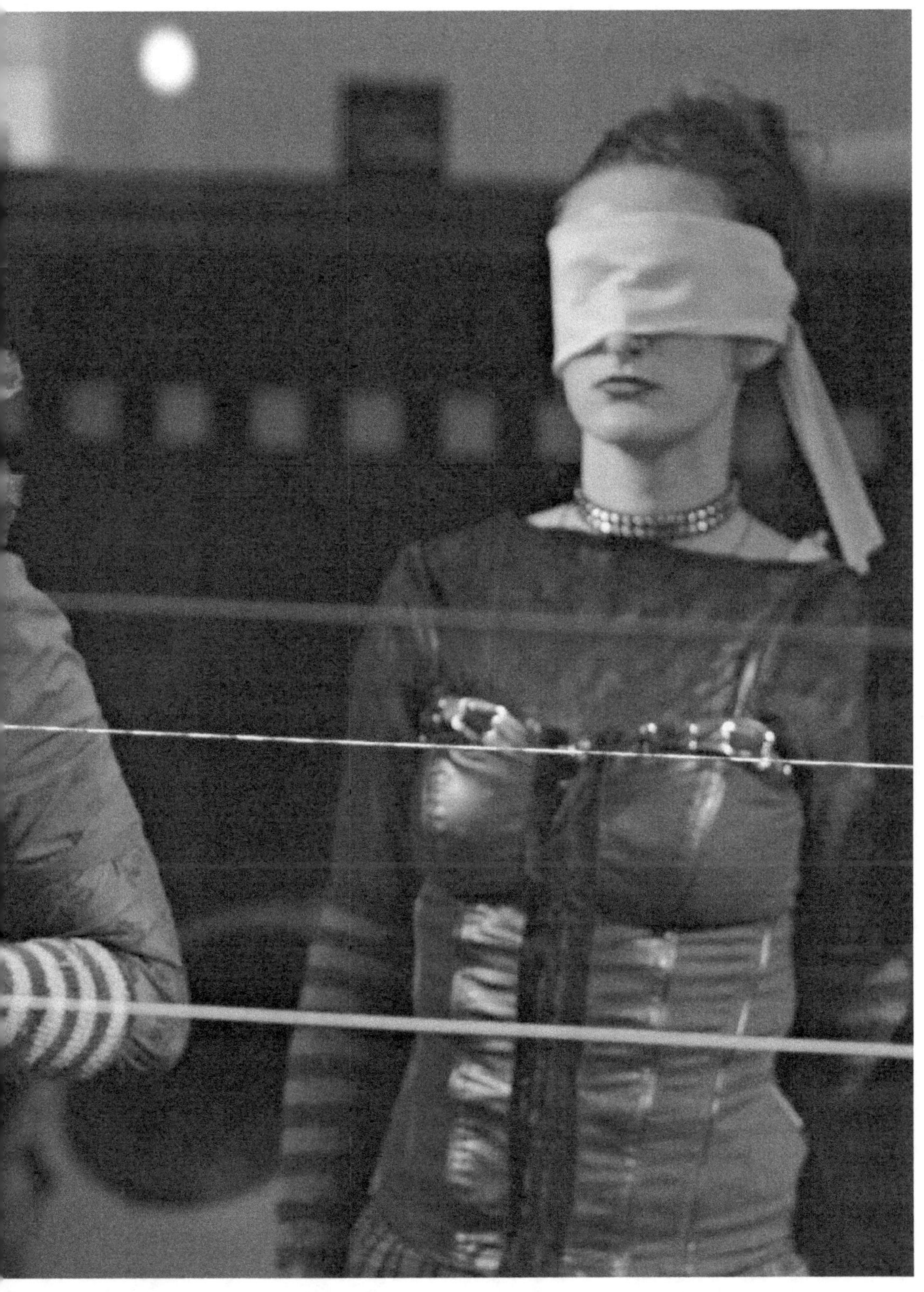

WAKE UP MR SLEEPY! YOUR UNCONSCIOUS MIND IS DEAD!

PRODUCTION HISTORY

Wake Up Mr. Sleepy! Your Unconscious Mind is Dead! Produced by the Ontological-Hysteric Theater at the Ontological at St. Mark's Theater, New York City. January 18 – April 22, 2007. Written, directed, & designed by Richard Foreman.

NYC LIVE CAST

Joel Israel: Tall Man
Chris Mirto: Short Man
Stefanie Neukirch: Girl in Pantsuit
James Peterson: Aviator
Stephanie Silver: Girl in Skirt

VOICES ON TAPE

Kate Manheim: Female Voice
Richard Foreman: Male Voice

LISBON FILM CAST

Samuel Alves
Carla Bolito
António Calpi
João Correia
María Duarte
Cândido Ferreira
Patrícia Galiano
Carla Galvão
Patrícia Leal
Tiago Manaia
Tita Morgado
Adelina Oliveira
João Pedreiro
André Teodósio

ATTENTION PLEASE

This evening's performance is the most accurate copy I am able to make of a strange theatrical event I viewed approximately one year ago when, against my will, I was forcibly seized and transported by a flying saucer to the alien planet Ax-e-tron. What surprised me most, perhaps, was that many of the elements of that alien performance – occurring light years from earth – seemed nevertheless to echo many of the concerns of our current earth-based mind-set. Though I can speculate as to why this might be so, I can at this date, offer no completely satisfactory explanation.

Richard Foreman

A large room with one projection screen on the upstage wall & another on the stage-left wall. On the corner of each screen is a letter. Throughout the play, the same film is projected on both screens. The printed words or phrases that appear on the screen throughout the play typically remain present for a brief period of time then vanish. Small panels are located at the bottom corner of each screen that contain electric candles – when the panels are opened, flares of light stream across the screen and into the stage area. Along the center of the bottom of the screen are four electric candles. There is a vertical black strip beneath the screen with white letters. Four black chairs with red cushions line the upstage wall.

The stage floor has one section covered with a large black and brown checkerboard pattern, another section with red, white, and black vertical stripes, and another with squares framing large white letters. The walls are covered with newspaper over which big letters have been loosely spray-painted in black.

At center stage is a small elevated boxing ring on top of a table draped with black velvet. There are chairs pushed closely in on both sides of the table. A few feet to stage left of the boxing ring, seated in an oddly extended sled-shaped wheelchair, is the torso of a life-like figure dressed in black with a high gold-studded collar, wearing a black sleep mask, and a black lace veil held in place by a small flat red cap and golden diadem-like brooch. Directed toward center stage, the length of the chair is parallel to the audience but the face of the figure is turned toward the audience throughout the play. Other objects situated about the stage include mannequin heads on columns, funeral vases with flowers, metal hurdles, red upholstered stools, and splayed-open books, several of which are displayed to face the audience by rods protruding from a striped metal bar that stretches the length of the front of the stage. A red toy airplane hangs near the stage-left screen, at times casting a shadow on it. Suspended above the wall at stage right and angled as if coming in for a landing, is a double-propeller brown airplane, suitable in size to fit an actual pilot, with its cockpit crammed full with a half-dozen plastic baby dolls, two with black wounds in their foreheads. And straddling the plane with legs wide apart and tightly holding rope in each hand that is tied to the middle of each wing, stands a curly-headed boy (or girl) wearing a white scarf and white Capri pants with a brown vest and sweater.

In the center of the boxing ring stands a placard that reads: RUNNING TIME: 1 HR 5 MIN.

Typesetting Key

00:00 (time stamp)

SCREEN – Screen tableaux

SCREEN LEGENDS

Live stage action

Voiceover

Sound & Music cue

raised-hyphen: word pronounced with elongated syllables

0:00

Music cue: *ethereal ambient sounds slowly increasing in volume.*

"WAKE UP MR. SLEEPY: YOUR UNCONSCIOUS MIND IS DEAD."

Deep Voice: 25 seconds. Seconds. 25 seconds.

Sound cue: *computerized distorted overlapping Russian dialogue.*

The Aviator enters and removes the Running Time placard from the boxing ring.

Sound cue: *repeating buzzer (5x).*

Stage goes dark. All actors enter. Girl in Skirt & Girl in Pantsuit walk to the upstage screen, place their hands upon it, then open the panels and stare into the light while the Tall Man & Short Man stare at the audience.

Sound cue: *smashing glass.*

Deep Voice: Ok, ok, are there any young children in the audience tonight? Yes? No?

Sound cue: *meditation bells.*

1:51 **SCREENS** – wipe to Diego's face. He is kneeling on the floor next to a red leather chair.

Sound cue: *chime, gong.*

?

2:01 **SCREENS** – wipe to Patricia's face. She is lapping up milk from a bowl, then turns and faces the camera.

Deep Voice: Ok, ok, are there any young children in the audience tonight? [Sound cue: *gong*] If there were young children here tonight [sound cue: *game show bells*] I would now be explaining to them specifically – [whisper] ev-ery-thing here is just for you.

All of the actors walk downstage to a waist-high, black vertical pole covered with white stripes. They point toward the small open books displayed at the front of the stage.

2:22 **SCREENS – FACES. WIPE TO:** newspaper being ripped open to reveal a girl's face.

Sound cue: *ringing phone, computer blip.*

SCREENS – FACES. GIRL: "Maybe it could happen in my lifetime. Tick tock, tick tock: it's broken and it can't be fixed."

As the ceiling lights flare on brightly, all of the actors swiftly turn toward stage right and point up at the propeller airplane, then spin around to their previous positions.

Deep Voice: I.E.

2:40 **SCREENS – THREE HEADS. WIPE TO:** full view of three women seated at a table with their hands stretched out in front of them. Their heads are wrapped with newspaper

and the table is covered with stuffed animals. A man walks behind them and exits.

?

Deep Voice: `Hav-ing been giv-en per-mis-sion to re-veal these se-crets. I am o-k with this in-for-ma-tion, so help me God.`

???

All of the actors turn about and position themselves around the boxing ring. They cover their faces with their hands. To the sound of a Chinese gong, they each quickly squat and make viewfinders with their hands then gaze through them.

Deep Voice: `Click.`

All of the actors widen their viewfinder hands.

Sound cue: *whirring noise.*

Short Man collapses to the floor.

3:16 **SCREENS — THREE HEADS: a person in a white jacket walks behind the women.**

Sound cue: *whirring noise.*

Tall Man, Girl in Pantsuit, and Girl in Skirt each collapse to the floor.

Screen lights and electric candles flare on.

Deep Voice: Be a-wake with-out know-ing it. [Whispered] Click. If it's bro-ken.

???

3:45 **SCREENS – THREE HEADS.** The girl in the center rips open the newspaper. GIRL: "Maybe it could happen in my life-time. Tick tock, tick tock: it's broken and it can't be fixed."

Light flare.

3:59 **SCREENS – THREE HEADS. WIPE TO:** close-up of the girl in the middle ripping open the newspaper.

Music cue: *ethereal chanting.*

SCREENS – THREE HEADS. GIRL: "Tick tock, tick tock: it's broken and it can't be fixed. Trust me, trust me."

Sound cue: *birds chirping.*

Girl in Pantsuit and Girl in Skirt point at the propeller airplane.

Deep Voice: The in-ven-tion of the air-plane, [sound cue: *computer blip*] a mortal blow to the unconscious.

Girl in Pantsuit and Girl in Skirt retract their hands.

4:22 **SCREENS – THREE HEADS. WIPE TO:** full view of the three girls. The girl on the left rips open the newspaper. GIRL: "Tick tock, tick tock: it's broken and it can't be fixed. Trust me, trust me."

Ceiling lights flare for an instant.

Sound cue: *bells, siren.*

As the stage lights go black, all of the actors rise from the ground then walk to the upstage screen and slap their hands on it.

NOW / NOT NOW

The actors sit in chairs in front of the screen and rub their hands together. A bright white light radiates outward from behind them.

Deep Voice: `In order to con-front, head on, the e-lu-sive re-al thing.`

Music cue: *violin/piano.*

Deep Voice: `Zip be-tween this, al-ways, double pro-ce-dure.`

`5:10`

Sound cue: *bell.*

All of the actors rise from their chairs, turn and stare at the upstage screen, then slowly return to their chairs.

???

5:20 **SCREENS – THREE HEADS:** a man in black walks behind the women then stands behind the girl on the left.

Sound cue: *computer blip, birds singing.*

Deep Voice: `When the world sees it-self, it does-n't.`

[flashing on & off]

X

5:34 **SCREENS – THREE HEADS:** a second man in a black suit enters and stands behind the girl in the center.

Deep Voice: `Tick, tock.`

5:37 **SCREENS – THREE HEADS.** Girl: "Tick tock, tick tock: it's broken, and it can't be fixed. Trust me; trust me."

All of the actors quickly rise from their chairs and slam their hands on the screen, then remove them. The actors in the center retreat while the remaining two open the panels in the screen and stare into them.

NOW (NOT NOW)

Sound cue: *gong.*

Girl in Pantsuit walks to center stage. With one hand, she points downwards at one of the miniature books; with the other, she points upwards. She stares into the audience, then slowly walks across the stage, stops, makes a 360° turn, then faces the audience and points upwards.

6:04 **SCREENS — THREE HEADS:** the men exit.

6:06 **SCREENS — THREE HEADS. CLOSE-UP OF:** Fatima ripping open the paper to reveal her face.

Deep Voice: `I.E. Men-tal.`

6:09 **SCREENS — WIPE TO: THREE HEADS.**

Girl in Pantsuit covers her face with her hands.

Voice: Lamp `must be re-plen-ished.`

6:12 **SCREENS — WIPE TO: OUTDOOR SCENE.**

Sound cue: *computer blip.*

Sound cue: *one inhalation/one exhalation, whip crack, game show bell.*

6:20 **SCREENS — WIPE TO:** a tableau of men and women seated at a table with white plates and half-full glasses. Behind them stand numerous people holding their hands over their faces. In the back, next to a series of windows, stands a woman in a black dress. In front of them is Maria, a woman with blonde hair wearing a blue-and-yellow jacket. Her left hand rests on her hip; her right hand is adjacent to her shoulder and closed in a fist.

Deep Voice (sung plangently): `Oh what did I do? What did I do?`

Sound cue: *electric gurgling noise.*

All of the actors spin around, place their hands on the upstage screen, then remove them and cover their faces with their hands.

THE UNCONSCIOUS MIND (NO MIND)

Girl in Pantsuit walks to stage left holding her hands out before her then grips a pole in front of the stage-left screen.

6:30 **SCREENS** – Maria shifts position, placing her right hand on her hip and her left hand adjacent to her shoulder, closed in a fist.

[flashing on & off]

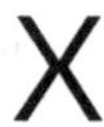

Sound cue: *loud banging, electric gurgling noise.*

SCREENS – **JOE**: "Tick tock, tick tock. It's broken and it can't be fixed."

Light flare.

7:05 **SCREENS** – **WIPE TO: TABLEAU**. The woman in black standing next to the windows begins slowly moving.

Sound cue: *gong, ding, game show bells, ringing phone.*

Voice: Dibitidoop.

Panel lights flare on and flood the screens. Tall Man walks to the stage-right side of the boxing ring & holds up a folder-sized, gold-framed hinged case with the letter E on its front. The other actors walk to the stage-left side of the ring, each holding up similar cases with letters (A, O, X). They point at the front of their cases while staring at the audience.

Voice: Tick tock.

Voice: Dibitidoop.

Deep Voice: This is for you, for you on-ly. Men-tal (seconds).

7:16 **SCREENS – WIPE TO: GROUP ONE #2.** Maria shifts back to holding her left hand on her hip while closing her right hand in a fist and holding it adjacent to her shoulder.

Sound cue: *buzzer, bell.*

ALWAYS YES ALWAYS (NO)

SCREENS – JOE: "Tick tock, tick tock. It's broken and it can't be fixed. What picture comes afterwards?"

Sound cue: *computerized distorted overlapping Russian voices.*

All of the actors open the hinged cases, which contain white blindfolds – they are adhered velcro-style to green velvet and stretch across the two panels of the case, at first resembling a treasured, secret piece of garment. The actors display the open cases to the audience.

7:43 **SCREENS** – Maria reverses her position.

"DO NOT TOUCH"

Sound cue: *computerized distorted overlapping Russian voices increase in volume.*

The actors sniff their blindfolds then remove them from their panels and hold them in the air.

8:00 **SCREENS** – all exit to the sound of plates dropping.

Sound cue: *whirring noise.*

Voice (enervated): Come back, come back, come back.

The actors wrap the blindfolds around their faces then encircle the boxing ring and clasp each other's hands.

8:16 **SCREENS – RE-WIPE TO: TABLEAU, GROUP ONE # 3.** Maria with left hand on hip and right hand enclosed in fist.

Deep Voice: Pre-ma-ture.

8:25

Deep Voice: If it's bro-ken.

Sound cue: *gong, electric gurgling noise increasing in volume, computer blip.*

Deep Voice: `If it's bro-ken. If it's bro-ken ...`

All of the actors release their clasped hands and walk downstage, then to stage right, where each of them retrieves a vase with plastic flowers and holds it aloft.

Sound cue: *electric gurgling noise.*

8:50 **SCREENS – TABLEAU**: group exits, save for the woman in the black dress, who stands against the back wall gyrating in slow motion. Maria shifts from position to position.

THE UNCONSCIOUS MIND: YES? (NO?)

Sound cue: *electric gurgling noise increases in volume.*

Deep Voice: `When the un-con-scious is dead.` [Sound cue: *plate smashing*] `Pre-ma-ture.`

9:14 **SCREENS – MARIA**: "May-be, [sound cue: *bell*] it could happen in my lifetime."

Aviator enters and takes the flowers from Tall Man and returns them to stage right.

3 3 3
3 3 3
3 3 3

9:28 [flashing on & off]

X

3	3	3
3	3	3
3	3	3

9:33 **SCREENS – GROUP RETURNS.** Joe places his glass on his plate.

The actors turn and face the stage-right wall, then turn around to face the screens. They lift their blindfolds in the air and point at the screens.

Deep Voice: `23 seconds, 22 seconds, 21 seconds, 20 seconds.`

10:08 **SCREENS – JOE: "Tick tock, tick tock. It's broken and it can't be fixed."**

Voice: `Tick tock.`

The actors storm around, stamping on the floor while holding their blindfolds aloft. THEY wave them in the air and chime in unison in high-pitched voices: "Good-bye! Good-bye! Bye!"

Voice: `Dibitidoop.`

Sound cue: *whip crack, chanting voices, whip crack, Chinese gong.*

10:30 **SCREENS – JOE:** "Tick tock, tick tock. It's broken and it can't be fixed."

Sound cue: *computerized thumping.*

The actors return their blindfolds to the lettered cases, place them on the ground, then hold their hands up in the air while gazing at the audience.

Deep Voice (with relish): Ah, it comes and goes.

Sound cue: *Chinese gong.*

10:45 **SCREENS – JOE:** "What picture comes afterwards?"

Sound cue: *bird noises.*

Deep Voice: In be-tween.

Sound cue: *bell.*

SCREENS – JOE: "What mental pictures come afterwards?"

Tall Man & Short Man come to downstage center, retrieve a miniature blond mannequin head, stare at the audience, then quickly walk to the screens and drop the heads on the ground.

Sound cue: *electric gurgling noise.*

Deep Voice: It will never hap-pen the way you want it to hap-pen.

[flashing on & off]

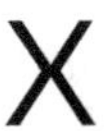

Sound cue: *game show bell, electric gurgling noise.*

Girl in Pantsuit walks to downstage center and holds her right finger to her temple as she stares into the audience.

Deep Voice: `In some dis-tant past, [whispers] un-con-scious.`

Sound cue: *electric gurgling noise increases in volume.*

Girl in Pantsuit places her left finger to her mouth. The actors all turn to face the screens and gesture as if praying to them, then turn back and place their hands on their heads.

11:10 **SCREENS – JOE: "Tick tock, tick tock. It's broken and it can't be fixed."**

Deep Voice: `Ah, it comes and goes.`

SCREENS – JOE: "What mental pictures come afterwards?"

All of the actors remove their hands from their heads & turn back toward the upstage screen.

Sound cue: *electric gurgling noise increases in volume, computer blip.*

11:38 **SCREENS – Maria shifts and reverses her position.**

Deep Voice: `But what is it that in fact hap-pened, hid-den, be-hind one's back?`

SCREENS – MARIA: "Maybe, it could happen in my lifetime."

Music cue: *brief emotional symphonic piece from Godard's* Contempt.

11:54 **SCREENS – JOE**: "Tick tock, tick tock. It's broken and it can't be fixed."

Deep Voice: To this, I'm tes-ti-fying.

SCREENS – JOE: "What mental pictures come afterwards?"

Sound cue: *loud door slam.*

Deep Voice: Ah, click. Click.

Music cue: *piece from Godard's* Contempt *increases in volume.*

All of the actors place their left forefingers beneath their left eye and pull down the skin as they stare at the audience, then swiftly flip their hands away and turn about. Girl in Skirt walks to the upstage screen and places her hands on it in a gesture of worship while the other actors crouch behind a pole at stage right and watch her.

12:20 Girl in Skirt walks to an inclined gangplank and shuffles up it toward the stage-left screen.

Deep Voice: Sup-pose I were to pos-tu-late.

Music cue: *piece from Godard's* Contempt.

SCREENS – ANTONIO: "Maybe it could happen in my lifetime. But I immediately lost consciousness."

[flashing on & off]

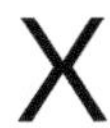

Overlapping Voices mumbling Swedenborg texts: ... a divine constant ... and that their interiors which see existing, are arranged to light ... but the thoughts and affections according to the form of heaven ... and consequently also their intelligence and wisdom would be seen above ... that the angels possess superior wisdom is further evidence ... their speech is the speech of wisdom, for it flows immediately as the wisdom of the ancients ... as thought flows from affection ... in its essence its divine truth ... nothing withdraws them from this light ... so their speech is thought and affection ... as is the case with man ... extraneous ideas into their thoughts ... that the speech of angels is their thoughts ... nothing withdraws them ... as is the case with man ... to maybe seen above ... another circumstance ... the angels also aspire to exalt the heavens above ... because of their existence ... which is its essence ... it defines good ... our desire ... which they see with their eyes ... wisdom ... [fades out].

13:20 **SCREENS** – Maria shifts to right. **WIPE TO: GROUP ONE #4.** MARIA: "Maybe it could happen in my lifetime." All exit, save for the woman in black and Maria.

Aviator holds an extended pointer with a large red circular tip toward the airplane while Tall Man, Girl in Pantsuit, and Short Man observe.

Deep Voice: The in-ven-tion of the airplane, a mor-tal BLOW to the un-con-scious.

Girl in Pantsuit is walking across a pole at the bottom of the stage-left screen. All turn to watch her as Girl in Skirt points at her from stage right. Silence.

13:50 **SCREENS** – Maria shifts to the left. The woman in black imitates her gestures in a slow but exaggerated manner.

Girl in Skirt turns toward stage right.

14:03 **SCREENS** – **MARIA**: "May-be it could happen in my life-time."

Sound cue: *bell.*

Deep Voice: `This might have been.`

Sound cue: *whip.*

Ceiling lights slowly fade out.

14:20 **SCREENS – SLOW-WIPE TO**: Maria.

Woman's Voice: `Wel-come to planet Ax-e-tron. Wel-come to planet Ax-e-tron.`

Sound cue: *chime (2x).*

Voice: `Dibitidoop.`

Music cue: *chanting voice.*

All actors exit, save for Girl in Skirt.

14:31 **SCREENS – WIPE TO: GROUP ONE #5**, paper heads.

Deep Voice: `Just suppose.`

Sound cue: *Chinese gong.*

Screen flares for an instant.

14:40 **SCREENS — ENTER TO: RIPPED HEADS. WIPE TO: GROUP ONE #6.**

Sound cue: *computerized distorted overlapping Russian voices.*

Deep Voice: `Un-con-scious. [Gravelly voice] ZIP be-tween this, al-ways, double pro-ce-dure.`

14:50 **SCREENS — WIPE TO:** Maria exiting. **QUICK WIPE TO: GROUP ONE # 7**

Sound cue: *thump.*

SCREENS — papers rise and all exit except for Diego.

Girl in Pantsuit completes her walk and stands at the far end of the screen. Short Man enters holding aloft a plate with playing cards, which Girl in Pantsuit takes, flinging single cards toward center stage. Tall Man walks toward her then stares and points at the upstage screen.

14:56 **SCREENS — WIPE TO:** Diego alone.

Deep Voice: `Ev-ery-thing here is al-most true.`

Sound cue: *whip.*

Light flash.

15:10 **SCREENS — WIPE TO:** Fatima asleep. Patricia throws miniature books.

Sound cue: *glass smashing.*

Tall Man, Short Man, & Girl in Skirt jump back, stare at the upstage screen, then take a playing card from the wall and display it to the audience.

15:18 **SCREENS — WIPE TO CLOSE-UP OF:** Patricia.

15:22 **SCREENS — WIPE TO: GROUP.** Patricia is laying out cards to play solitaire.

Voice: Dibitidoop.

Deep Voice: O-kay, o-kay, o-kay. Are there any young children in the audience tonight? Yes? No? [whisper] If it's bro-ken.

Sound cue: *thump.*

15:33 **SCREENS — WIPE TO: GROUP TWO.** A group of men and women sit, kneel, and stand before an ornate 18th-century lamp. Immediately to the right of the lamp stands the woman in the black dress. She is wearing a purple sweater and holds her right hand over her stomach while her left hand dangles at her side. Maria, who is blindfolded, is squatting immediately to the left of the lamp.

Sound cue: *chime.*

Woman's Voice (sings): Oh where, oh where is the un-conscious mind hi-ding? Oh where, oh where can it be?

THE UNCONSCIOUS MIND: (YES?) NO?

Sound cue: *plates smashing.*

[flashing on & off]

X

Girl in Skirt and Tall Man hold their hands in front of their faces and quickly slap the front and back of their hands together several times.

Voice: Eins, neun, neun, sechs, sollten abgeschleppt werden.

15:56 **SCREENS — WIPE TO: GROUP TWO.** A woman in a flower dress enters from screen-right and stares directly across at Fatima.

WHEN THE
UNCONSCIOUS
IS DEAD, WHERE
DOES IT HIDE?

Light bulb flash (2x).

All of the actors slowly raise their hands in the air in a gesture of worship.

WHEN THE
UNCONSCIOUS
IS DEAD, WHERE
DOES IT HIDE?

TALL MAN: O-k. Now.

Voice: Eins, neun, neun, sechs, sollten abgeschleppt werden.

TALL MAN: Wrong a-gain, swee-ty.

16:28 **SCREENS – FATIMA: "May-be it could happen in my life-time, but I immediately lost con-scious-ness."**

While staring at the stage-left screen, all of the actors slowly raise their hands in the air. Stage lights darken.

Sound cue: *humming noise.*

TALL MAN: Wrong a-gain.

Sound cue: *chime.*

Girl in Pantsuit lowers and raises her hands in the air then drops them and paces slowly in a circle. Light flares.

Sound cue: *electric gurgling noise.*

TALL MAN: More, more, more.

16:59 **SCREENS –** Fatima is blindfolded.

Sound cue: *electric gurgling noise increasing in volume.*

17:11 **SCREENS – WIPE TO CLOSE-UP OF:** hand on stomach.

17:22 **SCREENS – PAN TO:** mournful face.

Deep Voice: If not now, then, when?

17:28 **SCREENS – WIPE TO: GROUP #2.** FATIMA: "May-be it could happen in my life-time, but I immediately lost con-scious-ness."

Sound cue: *whirring, chime.*

Light flares on upstage screen.

Aviator enters and holds a series of numbered plates (1, 2, 3) in the air before the upstage screen, then drops each plate so they loudly strike the ground.

Sound cue: *chime.*

Deep voice: `Just sup-pose.`

Sound cue: *Chinese gong.*

18:02 **SCREENS** – a woman in a flower dress is blindfolded.

4

5

Voice: `Eins, neun, neun, sechs, sollten abgeschleppt werden.`

Girl in Skirt, Tall Man, and Short Man walk stage right, just below the propeller airplane, then hold their right hands next to their heads and point upwards, then exit.

Music cue: *religious hymns, cut quickly to baritone solo.*

18:28 **SCREENS – WOMAN in flower print dress: "Tick tock, tick tock. Trust me: it's broken and it can't be fixed."**

?

18:44

Deep Voice: `When the un-con-scious is dead.`

Sound cue: *computer blip, chime, electric gurgling noise.*

Girl in Pantsuit walks to center stage and stares into a light as she holds her hand against her stomach.

Deep Voice (whisper): `Click.`

19:19 **SCREENS – WOMAN in flower-print dress: "Tick tock, tick tock. Trust me: it's broken and it can't be fixed."**

Deep Voice: `Ahhh ... It comes and goes.`

Voice: `Dibitidoop. Beep.`

Deep Voice: `When I heard them say; when I heard them say, fail-ure is not per-mit-ted, then I knew this world was spir-i-tu-ally de-ple-ted.`

Sound cue: *thumping computerized industrial music.*

19:42 **SCREENS – VERY SLOW WIPE TO: GROUP #3.**

Girl in Pantsuit stares at the upstage screen and stretches her arms out perpendicular to the floor.

Ceiling lights swell on & off.

19:56 **SCREENS – GROUP TWO #3**: FATIMA: "Maybe it could happen in my lifetime, but I immediately lost consciousness."

SCREENS – GROUP TWO #3: WOMAN in flower-print dress: "Tick tock, tick tock. Trust me: it's broken and it can't be fixed."

Girl in Pantsuit runs to stage right and repeats her previous gesture.

20:17 **SCREENS – GROUP TWO #3**. Two doors open in the background. The men turn to look. The woman in the black dress & purple sweater collapses; another woman moves to help her. Fatima, Maria, and the woman in the flower-print dress remove their blindfolds and stare downwards.

All of the actors take pointers with round red tips and direct them at each screen.

20:44 **SCREENS – GROUP TWO #3**: FATIMA: "May-be it could happen in my lifetime, but I immediately lost con-sciousness."

All of the actors retract their pointers and turn away from the screens.

20:55

Sound cue: *door slamming.*

Deep Voice: A pen-ny for your deep-est thoughts ...

Sound cue: *deep breath, chime, whip crack, string pluck.*

Deep Voice: And I would explain that, soon after-wards, using a certain Dr. Sig-mund Freud [sound cue: *string pluck*] as a kind of fun-nel ... [in gravely voice] in order to confront, [sound cue: *electric gurgling noise*] head on, the e-lu-sive, re-al thing.

21:24 **SCREENS – GROUP TWO #3: FATIMA:** "May-be it could happen in my lifetime; may-be it could happen in my lifetime; may-be it could happen in my lifetime."

Sound cue: *electric gurgling noise increasing in volume.*

SCREENS – GROUP TWO #3: WOMAN in flower-print dress: "Tick tock, tick tock. Tick tock, tick tock. Tick tock, tick tock."

21:45 **SCREENS – DISSOLVE TO:** outside. A figure runs past.

Deep Voice (sung with a strong emphasis on each syllable):
Just like Lit-tle Red Ri-ding Hood, so mis-un-der-stood, so mis-un-der-stood.

21:52 **SCREENS – WIPE TO: GROUP TWO.**

Deep Voice: Just like Lit-tle Red Ri-ding Hood.

Sound cue: *curt opera loop.*

22:09 **SCREENS – DISSOLVE TO:** outside but closer.

22:18 **SCREENS – WIPE TO: GROUP TWO #4.** Men line each side of the open doorway and stare toward the camera.

Short Man walks off stage with his pointer.

22:22 **SCREENS – WIPE TO: GROUP TWO #5.** Women turn to look outside.

Deep Voice: I.E.

22:28 **SCREENS – DISSOLVE TO CLOSE-UP OUTSIDE:** a figure walks through a doorway and disappears.

Sound cue: *buzzer (3x).*

The remaining actors walk off stage, which is now completely dark.

22:42 **SCREENS – DISSOLVE BACK TO:** inside as women turn to look toward the open doors.

22:48 **SCREENS – WIPE TO: GROUP TWO #6.** A man walks in and blindfolds the woman in black with the purple sweater. She removes the blindfold.

Sound cue: *religious hymns, opera.*

22:55 **SCREENS – DISSOLVE TO:** face of woman on floor. She opens her eyes.

23:00 **SCREENS – JOE:** "Tick tock, tick tock."

Deep Voice: `Zip be-tween this, al-ways, dou-ble pro-ce-dure.`

23:08 **SCREENS – WIPE TO:** legs. A man in black is sitting with his arms folded across his chest; he is holding a book. Behind him is a sleeping woman whose legs are being held against a pole by a woman and a man. Two other figures crouch to the right of the frame.

Screen flare.

The actors stand in a line to the left of the upstage screen and stare at the audience.

23:19

1

Deep Voice: Click.

2

3

Deep Voice: Sup-pose I were to pos-tu-late.

Girl in Pantsuit & Girl in Skirt move to the stage-right wall and slam miniature blackboards against it then begin writing on them. Tall Man & Short Man repeat the same gesture.

Deep Voice: Just sup-pose.

Voice: Je dis tou-jours la vér-i-té.

Deep Voice: Un-a-voi-da-ble.

23:47 **SCREENS – JOE**: "Tick tock, tick tock. Maybe it could happen in my lifetime."

Deep Voice: Click.

Lights flare for an instant.

[flashing on & off]

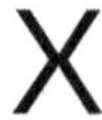

24:11 **SCREENS** – a girl in a purple jacket enters and whispers into David's ear.

24:16 **SCREENS** – David drops the book. The woman exits. David exits and is replaced by Antonio, an older man in a dinner jacket and black bowtie. He replicates David's position.

Sound cue: *loud banging noise, haunting humming sounds.*

Deep Voice: `Tick tock.`

All of the actors spin out toward the upstage screen and display their chalkboards to it.

Music cue: *opera.*

Deep Voice: `Tick tock.`

24:38 **SCREENS** – first girl enters and whispers to Antonio. Antonio drops his book.

Deep Voice: `Tick tock.`

24:50 **SCREENS** – David returns and resumes his position. The sleeping woman opens her eyes then closes them.

Sound cue: *computerized distorted overlapping Russian voices.*

"DO NOT TOUCH"

25:07 **SCREENS** – the woman in the purple jacket enters and whispers to David. He drops the book, then looks down. She exits. Antonio replaces David.

Deep Voice: Tick, tock.

Sound cue: *chime.*

All of the actors move to the boxing ring and place their chalkboards on it.

25:23 **SCREENS** – **JOE**: "Tick tock, tick tock. Maybe it could happen in my lifetime. Maybe."

Sound cue: *plates smashing.*

Voice: Eins, neun, neun, sechs, sollten abgeschleppt werden.

25:36 **SCREENS – LEFT-WIPE TO: GROUP TWO.**

Woman's Voice: Here on planet Ax-e-tron ...

25:40 **SCREENS – LEFT-WIPE TO: GROUP TWO.**

Voice: ... seconds.

Deep Voice: If it's broken ... If it's broken ... If it's broken.

SCREENS – woman whispers to Antonio.

Voice: 18 seconds, 17 seconds.

25:45 **SCREENS** – Antonio drops book; woman walks off.

Sound cue: *heavy breathing.*

[flashing on & off]

?

SCREENS – David enters, woman in flower-print dress hands him a book, which he clasps to his chest.

Voice: 16 seconds, 15 seconds.

SCREENS – woman enters and whispers to David. He drops the book. She exits. Antonio enters, woman in flower-print dress hands him a book; he clasps it to his chest.

Sound cue: *heavy breathing.*

Voice: 14 seconds, 13 seconds, 25, 24 seconds, 21 seconds ...

X

Music cue: *religious hymn.*

26:19 **SCREENS** – **JOE**: "Tick tock, tick tock. Maybe it could happen in my lifetime. Maybe."

Deep Voice: Ahhh ... It comes and goes.

Woman's Voice: Where ... Where is the un-con-scious mind hi-ding?

Music cue: *haunting voices.*

SCREENS – Sleeping **GIRL**: "Tick tock. It's broken and it can't be fixed. Trust me."

26:39

Deep Voice: `O-kay, o-kay. Are there any young children in the audience tonight?`

All of the actors rise and turn toward the propeller airplane and point at it, then turn around, grab their chalk boards, and hold them up to the airplane, then slam them on a black metal hurdle and begin feverishly writing on them.

Deep Voice (with a strong emphasis on each syllable): `I don't know, you don't know, no-bo-dy knows,` [sound cue: *plates breaking*] `no-bo-dy knows.`

THE UNCONSCIOUS MIND: (YES?) NO?

Deep Voice: `Re-mem-ber.`

Lights darken on stage.

27:00 **SCREENS** – **DISSOLVE TO**: sleeping girl. She opens her eyes. Dissolve back. The woman in the purple jacket enters, whispers in David's ear. He drops the book; she exits. Antonio replaces David.

All of the actors slam their chalkboards against the stage-right wall and write on them percussively.

Sound cue: *breathing.*

27:23 **SCREENS – Antonio receives the book. Repeat action. David enters.**

7

Deep Voice: Pre-ma-ture.

All of the actors untie the gravestone billboards from their backs then embrace them.

Deep Voice: Tick tock.

8

Deep Voice: 15 seconds. 14 seconds. (Tick tock.) 13 seconds.

Sound cue: *computerized industrial music.*

9

10

SCREENS – JOE: "Tick tock, tick tock. Maybe it could happen in my lifetime. Maybe. Maybe."

27:59 All of the actors spin around and stare at the propeller airplane, then at the upstage screen.

Sound cue: *chanting, sirens.*

Music cue: *opera loop.*

(DO NOT TOUCH)

28:13 **SCREENS – WIPE TO:** Patricia filming.

Sound cue: *computerized thumping industrial music; computerized distorted overlapping Russian voices.*

Deep Voice: `I do forget if there are children who have –`

Deep Voice (sung): `I hear you knock-in', but you can't get in.`

28:23 **SCREENS – WIPE TO TABLEAU OF:** a woman with an eye patch & a woman with a purple headwrap sitting down, both being embraced from behind by a man.

Sound cue: *Chinese gong, whirring noise.*

Aviator and Tall Man enter, slam large billboards painted with Tutankhamen onto the metal hurdle, step on them, then point at the propeller airplane.

28:35

Deep Voice: Oh, figh-ter air-planes, [whispered] in be-tween.

Sound cue: *resonating chimes.*

Girl in Skirt places her hands on the Aviator's shoulders, then moves around him and prays under the airplane. The Aviator turns toward the boxing ring, stretching his arms in front of himself.

Music cue: *German lieder, opera loop.*

28:49 **SCREENS – LEFT-WIPE TO: cover rear couple.**

Girl in Skirt walks to the right of the boxing ring and stares at the audience.

Sound cue: *chime, whirring noise.*

Tall Man and Short Man stand before the Egyptian bill-boards and stare at the stage-left screen.

Sound cue: *chime.*

29:15 **SCREENS – figures enter with sheets and drape them over each couple.**

Girl in Pantsuit and Girl in Skirt walk to the gravestone billboards, then lay on them and hold their hands over their chests and pray.

29:30 **SCREENS – WIPE TO: Egon # 2. The rear couple is covered with a white sheet.**

Deep Voice: `If hap-pi-ness en-fol-ded hu-man be-ings, then hu-man be-ings would find it dif-fi-cult to im-prove them-selves.`

Music cue: *opera loop, whirring noise.*

Girl in Pantsuit & Girl in Skirt rise from the billboards, move to either side of the boxing ring, then wrap their lower bodies in black fabric. Tall Man and Short Man blindfold them.

30:02 **SCREENS – pan out to reveal figures with their heads wrapped in paper on either side of each couple.**

Sound cue: *computer blip, whirring noise, chime.*

Short Man and Tall Man take the Tutankhamen panels off stage.

Deep Voice: `Things bite back.`

Sound cue: *whiplash, whirring noise.*

Music cue: *opera loop.*

30:21 **SCREENS – WIPE TO: wrapping paper around heads. The white fabric is removed from the couple in the rear.**

Music cue: *lieder.*

Short Man and Tall Man open the panels in the upstage screen and stare into them.

30:27 **SCREENS – WIPE BACK TO: wrapped heads.**

30:36 **SCREENS – WIPE TO**: Egon #4. Man tears paper open.

Deep Voice: If hap-pi-ness en-fol-ded hu-man be-ings –

30:52 **SCREENS – FANTASIA. EGON**: "Tick tock, tick tock. I hear you knock, but you can't get in."

Deep Voice: Lamp must be re-plen-ished.

Sound cue: *meditation bell.*

Music cue: *Beethoven sonata.*

Deep Voice: Lamp must be re-plen-ished. I.E.

31:14 **SCREENS** – Samuel tears open paper.

Music cue: *Beethoven sonata.*

Short Man & Tall Man cover the heads of Girl in Pantsuit and Girl in Skirt with white cone-hat masks, then the girls place their fingers just beneath their eyeholes. Short Man & Tall Man cover their own heads with the same masks and repeat the finger-to-eye gesture.

Deep Voice: One path leads to qual-i-ty.

31:25 **SCREENS – SAMUEL**: "Tick tock, tick tock. May-be it could hap-pen in my life-time. Trust me."

31:40 **SCREENS – WIPE TO CLOSE-UP OF**: Samuel.

Music cue: *Beethoven sonata.*

SCREENS – SAMUEL: "May-be it could hap-pen in my life-time. Trust me."

31:51 **SCREENS – WIPE TO**: sleeping group. A woman is lying on a hospital bed in an ornate room with lacquered walls. She is blanketed with a Turkish carpet and is holding a plate in her hand. She is surrounded by other figures, all gazing at her, except for Fatima, who holds her hands over her face. One woman stands directly behind her, patting her head with a cloth. In the background is another woman on a hospital bed.

Sound cue: *humming noise, snoring, organ drone.*

Deep Voice: One path leads to quality, but a second path runs par-a-llel to that first path. [Sound cue: *chime.*] Two pla-ces at once. To this I tes-ti-fy.

Girl in Pantsuit removes her white cone-hooded mask, exits, then returns and stands near Short Man & Tall Man.

32:18 **SCREENS** – eyes of patting girl look up.

Sound cue: *humming noise & organ drone.*

Deep Voice: He or she in fact, de-nied, having spo-ken such words.

32:48

Music cue: *Beethoven sonata.*

Girl in Pantsuit enters with giant scissors and opens them above Short Man's head, then does the same to Tall Man, after which they remove their masks.

SCREENS – JOE: "May-be it could happen in my life-time."

Sound cue: *chime.*

32:55 **SCREENS — WIPE TO CLOSE-UP OF:** sleeping girl. She opens her eyes.

Short Man then removes the cone-hat mask of Girl in Skirt, then both turn to stare at the upstage screen.

Deep Voice: `Ahhh, this will make you feel bet-ter.`

Music cue: *string pluck, violin.*

33:13 **SCREENS — DISSOLVE TO CLOSE-UP OF:** knife on wrist.

Sound cue: *whirring noise.*

Deep Voice: `Bro-ken like.`

Stage flooded with bright light. All of the actors turn & stare at the ceiling.

Woman's Voice: `Here, on planet Ax-e-tron, the world of i-ma-gi-na-tion is the world of the imagination.`

Tall Man and Girl in Pantsuit enter with giant open scissors, lift them above their heads, then point them at the stage-left screen.

33:25 **SCREENS — WIPE TO: SLEEP # 2.**

Music cue: *chorus-like eerie hum.*

Deep Voice (sings with a strong emphasis on each syllable): `Just like Lit-tle Red Ri-ding Hood, so mis-un-der-stood, so mis-un-der-stood.`

Music cue: *20s jazz.*

Bright lights flood the stage. Short Man and Girl in Skirt enter with scissors framed in glass.

33:43

LOOK WHAT THE UNCONSCIOUS MIND HATH WROUGHT (DEAD / NOT DEAD)

Voice: Eins, neun, neun, sechs, sollten abgeschleppt werden.

Tall Man & Girl in Pantsuit slowly pivot around clockwise with their giant scissors till they are facing the upstage screen, cut with their scissors in the air, then turn back and point their scissors at the propeller airplane.

33:51 **SCREENS – JOE**: "Maybe it could happen in my lifetime. Trust me. Trust me."

Deep Voice: When the un-con-scious is dead –

Voice: Dibitiboop. Eeep!

Deep Voice: The Fighter airplanes say – we are a-lone on earth, [sound cue: *Chinese gong*] we are blind, we are deaf, with no tac-tile sen-sa-tion.

Upstage screen is flooded with bright light. The lights on the propeller airplane darken. Girl in Pantsuit and Tall Man step backwards and cut once with their scissors.

Voice: Dibitidoop. Eeep!

34:10

Deep Voice: If it's bro-ken, if it's bro-ken.

Sound cue: *smashing glass.*

Voice: Dibitidoop.

Deep Voice: When the unconscious is dead, use please the hu-man mind to dig up, from the depths, that men-tal baf-fle ma-chine, uncovering the sleeping giant whose name must nev-er be spo-ken.

Music cue: *20s jazz.*

The lights on the propeller airplane are shut off completely.

34:30

LOOK WHAT THE UNCONSCIOUS MIND HATH WROUGHT.

Voice: Eins, neun, neun, sechs, sollten abgeschleppt werden.

Girl in Pantsuit and Tall Man do 20s style dance to the music, swaying back and forth with their scissors as they proceed toward the stage-right wall.

Voice: Lamp must be re-plen-ished. Lamp must be re-plen-ished. Lamp must be re-plen-ished.

Sound cue: *smashing glass (3x).*

Short Man and Girl in Skirt raise their hands in the air before the propeller airplane.

Voice: `Eins, neun, neun, sechs, sollten abgeschleppt werden.`

Music cue: *mournful clip from Godard's Contempt.*

Girl in Pantsuit turns and points at Short Man & Girl in Skirt, then moves around them and points at the upstage screen.

34:56

?

Girl in Pantsuit moves to downstage center, points at one of the miniature books which line the front barricade, then turns back to the upstage screen and points.

35:10 **SCREENS** — Maria enters to blindfold Joe.

Deep Voice: `Re-mem-ber.`

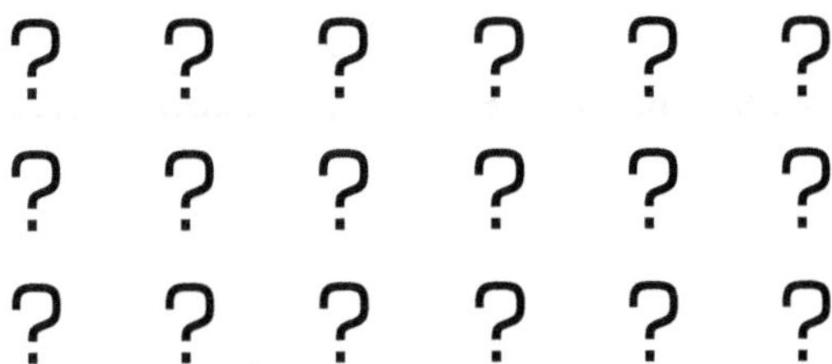

Deep Voice: `Things bite back. Risk it.`

35:13 **SCREENS** – Maria exits. **JOE**: "Maybe it could happen in my lifetime. Trust me. Trust me."

Music cue: *mournful clip from Godard's Contempt increasing in volume.*

Deep Voice (sung): `Just like Little Red Ri-ding Hood, so mis-un-der-stood, so mis-un-der-stood.`

35:22 **SCREENS** – men begin to sneak in, entering the background.

Girl in Skirt and Short Man enter with a long whip and stand in front of the upstage screen, make choking noises, fall to the ground, then rise and open the panels in the upstage screen, displaying the electric candles within.

35:38 **SCREENS** – **WOMAN** wiping girl's forehead: "Tick tock, tick tock, just like little Miss Red Riding Hood, so misunderstood."

Deep Voice: `I.E., suppose I were to postulate, just sup-pose.`

Tall Man and Girl in Pantsuit approach Short Man and Girl in Skirt, take the snake-shaped flytraps from them, then walk to downstage center and hold them in the air between their scissors as if to cut them.

Screen turns off.

Voice: `I.E., things bite back.`

Voice: `Eins, neun, neun, sechs, sollten abgeschleppt werden.`

Deep Voice: `I.E. Yes, no.`

Voice: `Eins, neun, neun, sechs, sollten abgeschleppt werden.`

35:50 **SCREENS** – **DISSOLVE TO CLOSE-UP OF**: sleeping woman.

Girl in Pantsuit runs to stage right, stands on a platform, stretches her arms out toward the propeller airplane as she stares into the audience. Short Man holds her waist and gazes at the upstage wall.

Music cue: *mournful music.*

Deep Voice: `O-kay, O-kay ...`

`36:01` **SCREENS — WIPE TO:** Fatima looking.

Sound cue: *chime.*

Deep Voice: `If there were young children here tonight, I would now be explaining to them specifically ...`

`36:06` **SCREENS — WIPE TO: SLEEP #3.**

Deep Voice, continuing: `... that once upon a time ...`

`36:11` **SCREENS — WIPE THROUGH TO: SLEEP #4.**

Deep Voice, continuing: `... a lone-ly man cried out: [whisper] CLICK ... If it's bro-ken, if it's bro-ken.`

Four blocks of light pulse on and off beneath the upstage screen.

`36:21`

Sound cue: *flying saucer hum.*

Tall Man walks to downstage center and holds his hand over a light. Short Man is standing behind him. Girl in Pantsuit approaches with two white plates and holds them in front of her chest. Tall Man points toward them.

Voice: Eins, neun, neun, sechs, sollten abgeschleppt werden.

Girl in Pantsuit places one of the white plates on a stand before Tall Man and another on a stand before the boxing ring, then exits. Short Man places his hand over his breast and stands at attention.

36:28 **SCREENS** – Fatima uncovers her eyes.

Sound cue: *ringing phone.*

Tall Man and Short Man remove the plates from the stands and begin polishing them with the white blindfolds, hold them up, then place them back on the stands and place their middle fingers in the center of the plate. After a moment they quickly remove their fingers, then jut them at the upstage screen.

Sound cue: *chime (2x).*

Tall Man & Short Man kneel before the plates and place their hands on either side of the stands.

Sound cue: *flying saucer hum, slowly increasing in volume then fading out.*

36:52 **SCREENS** – WOMAN, as she pats sleeping girl's forehead: "Tick tock, tick tock, just like little Miss Red Riding Hood, so misunderstood." Fatima covers her eyes again with her hands.

Deep Voice: Suppose I were to pos-tu-late. [Sound cue: *chime*] Here is a world trying to run fast-er than the un-con-scious mind. But, who wins such a race?

"ALL BETS ARE OFF"

Sound cue: *ringing phone.*

Deep Voice: `All bets are off, all bets are off. [Whispered] Click.`

Tall Man & Short Man cover their faces with plates that have red-and-white striped bull's-eyes painted on them.

Bright lights flood stage right, where Girl in Pantsuit is now standing next to a large rectangular billboard. Girl in Skirt is kneeling before it and holding her hands together praying. Girl in Pantsuit moves to the front of the billboard and holds her hands together in the same manner.

Sound cue: *computerized distorted overlapping Russian voices.*

SCREENS – Maria leans in to remove Joe's blindfold.

37:49 **SCREENS** – Maria exits.

"ALL BETS
ARE OFF"

"ALL BETS
ARE OFF"

Deep Voice: `I.E. If it's bro-ken.`

?

Tall Man & Short Man walk to the upstage screen and hold their plates up to it.

38:08 **SCREENS – WIPE TO: SLEEP #5.** Plate falls.

Sound cue: *meditation bell and organ, heavy breathing.*

Deep Voice: Risk it. If it's bro-ken. Risk it.

Tall Man and Short Man walk to downstage center and hold the plates against their chests. Girl in Pantsuit and Girl in Skirt place their hands over the plates, take them from Tall Man and Short Man, then clean them with the blindfolds and hand them back.

Deep Voice: Un-a-voi-da-ble.

38:28 **SCREENS – WIPE TO: ROPE.** A group of five men squat on the ground, each with a woman sitting over their shoulders and holding their faces.

Sound cue: *chime.*

Music cue: *Beethoven sonata.*

?

38:36 **SCREENS – WIPE TO CLOSE-UP OF:** David.

Deep Voice: Just sup-pose. [Music cue: *mystic music*] Ahhh ... It comes and goes.

Music cue: *chanting.*

Tall Man and Girl in Skirt turn toward the upstage screen and stare at it.

Deep Voice: `Un-a-voi-da-ble.`

38:50 **SCREENS — SLOW WIPE TO: ROPE #2.**

Girl in Pantsuit and Girl in Skirt walk toward the stage-right wall, stand before a large rectangular white screen with letters in each corner (X, S/K, Q, T), reach up, grab a string, then pull it down. While holding the string in their hands, they make a slow circular turn until they revolve completely, then place their left hands on the screen.

Music cue: *Beethoven sonata.*

Voice: Lamp `must be re-plen-ished.`

Music cue: *Beethoven sonata.*

SCREENS: a taut rope that the women hold is stretched across the screen. DIEGO: "Tick tock, tick tock; I immediately lost consciousness."

Deep Voice: `Not quite. In fact, it is the little children who are hi-ding, in hi-ding places –`

39:19 **SCREENS — WIPE TO: ROPE #3.**

Deep Voice, continuing: `... they who will understand me I think, and so I say ...`

Sound cue: *smashing plates.*

Tall Man & Short Man spin around quickly and point at the upstage screen.

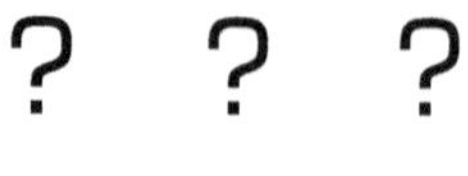

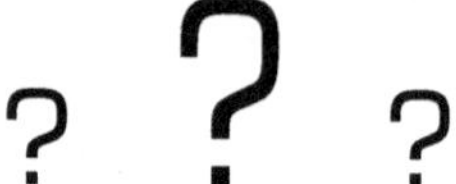

Short Man collapses.

Sound cue: *smashing plates.*

Music cue: *chorus of haunting voices.*

Tall Man collapses.

Sound cue: *plates smashing, humming, plates smashing.*

Deep Voice: Me, me, me. Me, me, me.

39:45

DEAD / NOT DEAD ?

39:48 **SCREENS – DISSOLVE TO**: women lifting the rope over their heads.

Deep Voice (sung): Oh what did I do, what did I do?

Deep Voice: Guess what, it really happened to me when I was a kid. I was a young person dreaming, and I climbed out of a pit in this dream,

SCREENS – **DAVID**: "I hear you knocking, knock, knock, knock – but you can't get in."

Deep Voice, continuing: ... a pit dug into the earth, and as I climbed up from the pit, and looked over the edge of the pit, there over my head was an airplane flying (I hear you knock-in', but you can't get in) low, and in that airplane were people, people looking at me, people jammed into the cockpit looking at me –

Deep Voice: I hear you knock-ing, knock, knock, knock – but you can't get in.

40:10

Music cue: *chorus of haunting voices.*

?

Deep Voice, continuing: ... and ([sung] Oh what did I do, what did I do?) from their eyes, from their eyes into my body.

Short Man stands up and holds his hand over a miniature book and points at it.

Deep Voice: This is for you, for you on-ly.

40:18 **SCREENS** – Women start to look up. **DAVID**: "I hear you knocking [sound cue: *knocking sound*]: knock, knock, knock – but you can't get in."

Sound cue: *chime.*

Girl in Pantsuit & Girl in Skirt keep making slow circular turns before the white screen.

Deep Voice: Guess what, it really happened to me when I was a kid. I was a young person dream-ing, and I climbed out of a pit in this dream, a pit dug into the earth, and as I climbed up from the pit, and looked over the edge of the pit, there over my head was an airplane fly-ing low, and in that air-plane, peo-ple, peo-ple looking at me, peo-ple jammed into the cockpit looking at me, and from their eyes, from their eyes into my bo-dy.

SCREENS – DIEGO: "Tick tock, tick tock; I immediately lost consciousness."

?

Deep Voice (sung): Oh what did I do, what did I do?

Sound cue: *knocking, eerie noises.*

Girl in Pantsuit and Girl in Skirt stare at the white screen while holding their hands on their heads. They remain in position, perfectly still.

41:13 **SCREENS** – the men rise and fall one by one.

Voice: Dibitidoop. Dibitidoop. Dibitidoop.

41:14 **SCREENS** – last fall.

Sound cue: *humming noise.*

?

Short Man and Tall Man run to the upstage screen and open the panels, then close them.

Woman's Voice: Here, on planet Ax-e-tron, no dis-tinc-tion is made be-tween i-deas that are good for you [sound cue: *chime*], and i-deas that are bad for you.

Deep Voice: Some people [sound cue: *chime*] no lon-ger make the dis-tinc-tion be-tween what they un-der-stand, and –

41:41 [flashing on & off]

X

Deep Voice, continuing: ... what they do not un-der-stand, and have ea-si-ly, therefore, solved their ma-jor psy-cho-logical problems.

Short Man & Tall Man open the screen panels and light flares out of them. Leaping back, they place their hands on their heads and begin spinning around in circles.

41:48 **SCREENS – WIPE TO: ROPE #4.** Two men rise and then sit, rise and then sit.

Sound cue: *haunting chant.*

[flashing on & off]

X

Deep Voice: Me, me, me. Me, me, me. [Whispered] Knock, knock, let me in! I am here to re-in-flate the bal-loon of human con-scious-ness.

Music cue: *carousel circus tune.*

Tall Man and Short Man continue spinning madly in circles, then stop & hold their hands toward the screen.

Deep Voice (yelling with a strong emphasis on each syllable): I don't know, you don't know, no-bo-dy knows, nobo-dy knows, no-bo-dy knows.

The panel lights flare off.

42:23 **SCREENS – DAVID**: "I hear you knocking, knock, knock, knock –"

42:25 **SCREENS – WIPE TO: ROPE #5.** Men rise and fall.

Sound cue: *whirring noise, chime.*

Deep Voice: I do for-get if there are children left be-hind, that I would be able to explain things to such young and pli-a-ble minds. And I would ex-plain, that soon afterwards, using a certain Dr. Sig-mund Freud as a kind of fun-nel –

Panel lights flare on again, then flare for an instant. Tall Man and Short Man close the panels.

Sound cue: *ding; machine-gun blasts.*

Music cue: *haunting ambient sounds.*

42:41 **SCREENS – WIPE TO: ROPE #6.** A group of women standing against the wall, each holding onto a part of a long rope, raise it from behind themselves and over their heads to hold it in front of themselves.

Deep Voice, continuing: ... this dead god's uni-verse did thrust forward a sub-sti-tute rep-re-sen-ta-tion. [Whispered] Ac-cur-ate di-ag-nosis.

42:55 **SCREENS – WIPE TO: ROPE #7.** Women with hands on chest, two men return to sit.

Deep Voice (yelling with a strong emphasis on each syllable):
I don't know, you don't know, no-bo-dy knows,
no-bo-dy knows, no-bo-dy knows!

Music cue: *haunting ambient sounds increasing in volume.*

Sound cue: *loud chime, machine gun blasts.*

12131415
16171819
12131415
16171819

Sound cue: *Chinese gong, ringing phone.*

43:18

Deep Voice: Guess what, it really happened to me when I was a kid. I was a young person dream-ing, and I climbed out of a pit [music cue: *eerie chanting & chime*] in this dream, a pit dug into the earth.

Sound cue: *chorus of haunting voices.*

Short Man lowers the white lettered screen from the ceiling and carries it out as Girl in Pantsuit and Girl in Skirt recline back on poles, point their fingers to their heads, and gaze at the audience.

Deep Voice: The per-fect i-dea [sound cue: *haunting chime*]. Men-tal. The per-fect ... feel-ing. [Sound cue: *chime*] Click now for ad-di-tion-al hap-pi-ness.

Girl in Pantsuit and Girl in Skirt walk to the upstage screen and place their hands on it, remove them, then open the panels, out of which bright light emits.

Music cue: *Beethoven sonata.*

43:53 **SCREENS — ROLL UP TO: SIDE VIEW OF ROPE.** Men stand, women already up.

Girl in Pantsuit places a chair sideways on the boxing ring.

[flashing on & off]

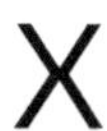

44:05 **SCREENS – VERY SLOW WIPE IN TO:** Maria with a white cap. She is sitting in a chair and holding her hands in front of her as if looking into a mirror. She turns to look. A man is sitting next to her in a red chair while another kneels on the floor gazing at her.

Short Man wheels a stand to the right of the boxing ring, then stands on it. Tall Man places the pointed mask on his head.

Girl in Pantsuit makes a circular turn.

Deep Voice: `Men-tal.`

Girl in Pantsuit and Girl in Skirt clap twice.

Sound cue: *ringing phone, Chinese gong.*

Short Man turns in a circle then places his fingers on the eyeholes of the mask.

44:23 **SCREENS – MARIA:** "Knock, knock, knock. The stone that rolls up the hill back-wards, is called the e-vil one –"

Sound cue: *chime.*

44:41

Deep Voice (gravelly tone): `This, might have been, the won-der-ful ad-ven-tures of the wo-man, who did not dance.`

Lights slowly brighten.

Girl in Skirt, Tall Man, and Girl in Pantsuit raise stuffed animals above their heads, then drop them and begin dancing, making flamenco steps, then carry the stuffed animals to Short Man and place them in his hands.

Music cue: *haunting melancholic violin.*

Sound cue: *idea bell.*

44:51 **SCREENS** — Maria completes turn back to mirror.

Deep Voice: `The stone that rolls up the hill back-wards, is called –`

45:02 **SCREENS** — Two men with their heads wrapped in paper enter. Antonio turns out toward the camera.

Girl in Skirt, Tall Man, and Girl in Pantsuit pick up pieces of newspaper, sit down on chairs to the side and behind the boxing ring, then wrap their heads with the paper.

Short Man enters wearing white cone-hat mask and carrying stuffed animals. He faces the audience, then turns back toward the upstage screen.

45:42 **SCREENS** — Maria starts to turn out. Diego turns out toward the camera.

Sound cue: *computerized machine gun noise at low volume.*

Deep Voice: `Suppose I were to pos-tu-late.`

Short Man drops the stuffed animals.

Music cue: *violin/piano, computerized machine gun noise slowly increasing in volume.*

46:01 **SCREENS** — DIEGO: "May-be, it could hap-pen in my lifetime."

Short Man removes the blindfold then carries the stuffed animals stage right and places them inside a red cabinet, then quickly crouches and stares at the upstage screen.

Deep Voice: I am o-kay with this in-for-ma-tion, so help me God. [Whispered] Click. Re-mem-ber the truth is nev-er amusing. [Sound cue: *buzzer.*] [Yelling] I don't know, you don't know, no-bo-dy knows, no-bo-dy knows, no-bo-dy knows. Knock, knock, let me in. (Ohhh, what did I do, what did I do?) I am here to re-in-flate the bal-loon of human con-scious-ness.

Music cue: *20s jazz.*

SCREENS – Diego completes look back at Maria.

Sound cue: *buzzer, haunting voices.*

46:40 **SCREENS – WIPE TO CLOSE-UP OF:** Maria.

Girl in Skirt, Tall Man, and Girl in Pantsuit remove the paper from their heads and crush it into balls as they walk to the right of the boxing ring then turn toward the upstage screen and extend their arms toward it and point at it.

46:46 **SCREENS – WIPE TO: SIT #2.** Men remove paper from their heads and exit.

Sound cue: *chorus of haunting voices.*

Deep Voice: Dogs weep-ing without think-ing.

Music cue: *20s jazz continues.*

Girl in Pantsuit, Tall Man, Short Man, and Girl in Skirt each slap their hands together then walk to different points around the stage and stare into the sky.

Voice: Eins, neun, neun, sechs, sollten abgeschleppt werden.

Girl in Skirt, Tall Man, Short Man, and Girl in Skirt all swing their hands around and slap their buttocks then turn around and quickly rub their hands together. Aviator enters and places a red bucket on the ground next to Tall Man, who places one foot in the bucket then begins dancing with his other foot.

Deep Voice (yelling with a strong emphasis on each syllable): I don't know, you don't know, no-bo-dy knows, noooobo-dy knows, no-bo-dy knows.

Deep Voice: No no no no no no no no no no no no no.

OH WHERE OH WHERE IS THE UNCONSCIOUS MIND HIDING?

Voice: Eins, neun, neun, sechs, sollten abgeschleppt werden.

Short Man runs at the stage-left screen then shakes his hands wildly in the air and falls to the ground. General mayhem.

Girl in Skirt, Tall Man, and Girl in Pantsuit each hold their hands to the sides of their heads and move them up and down while quickly tilting their heads back and forth while Short Man rises from the ground and points at one of the miniature books lining the front of the stage.

Deep Voice: Rock-a-bye-baby. Au-to-ma-ti-cally real. [sound cue: *chorus of haunting voices.*] Yes. No. [Singing] Rock-a-bye-baby. Au-to-ma-ti-cally real.

SCREENS – DIEGO: “Maybe it could happen in my lifetime.”

SCREENS – Diego turns back, Maria turns out.

Girl in Pantsuit, Tall Man, and Girl in Skirt each grab a black bucket and place them on stands then swiftly thrust their fingers at the center of the overturned buckets numerous times then place the buckets over their heads.

Voice: Dibitidoop. Eeep.

Deep Voice: Hi-ding it, because no-body was, look-ing at it.

47:40 SCREENS – Maria completes turn out toward the camera.

Deep Voice: Men-tal te-lep-athy cer-tain-ly.

Short Man points at the upstage screen, grunts.

Sound cue: *ringing phone, computerized thumping industrial rock slowly increasing in volume.*

Short Man runs to the upstage screen, closes one of the lighted panels, then opens it and retreats.

Overlapping Voices mumbling Swedenborg texts: ... and that their interiors which see existing, are arranged to light ... but the thoughts and affections according to the form of heaven ... and consequently also their intelligence and wisdom would be seen above ... that the angels possess superior wisdom is further evidence ... their speech is the speech of wisdom, for it flows immediately as the wisdom of the ancients ... as thought flows from affection ... in its essence its divine truth ... nothing withdraws them from this light ... so their speech is thought and affection ... as is the case with man ... extraneous ideas into their thoughts ... that the speech of angels is their thoughts ... nothing withdraws them ... as is the case with man ... to maybe seen above ... another circumstance ... the angels also aspire to exalt the heavens above ... because of their existence ... which is its essence ... it defines good ... our desire ... which they see with their eyes ... wisdom ... [fades out].

48:22 **SCREENS – DISSOLVE TO:** Maria & David sitting on bicycles. They are each being embraced from behind.

Sound cue: *chime.*

Music cue: *violin/piano.*

Deep Voice: Click.

SCREENS – MARIA: "Knock, knock, knock. The stone that rolls up the hill back-wards, is called the evil one –"

Music cue: *short repetitive loop, like a skipping record, of a man singing in French.*

[flashing on & off]

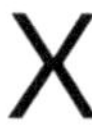

Deep Voice: The stone that rolls up the hill back-wards is called –

48:44 **SCREENS** – Antonio turns to camera. A man & woman in black enter and walk into the background and begin kissing. ANTONIO: "Tick tock, it's broken and it can't be fixed."

Voice: `Where is –`

GIRLS: Hello. Hello.

48:56 **SCREENS** – couple embracing in the rear. Antonio looks back at Maria.

Music cue: *computerized thumping industrial rock.*

Overlapping Voices mumbling Swedenborg texts again.

TALL MAN: He-he-he-hel-lo.

Sound cue: *ringing phone, computerized industrial music.*

As the Aviator walks by Girl in Skirt, Tall Man, & Girl in Pantsuit, he hands each a doll and a stuffed animal, then exits stage right. Aviator and an assistant return with the Tutankhamen billboards and hook them on the black railing to the right of the boxing ring, forming two ramps.

After dropping the stuffed animals, Girl in Skirt and Girl in Pantsuit approach the ramps. They are carrying the long-legged dolls, dangling them by the legs, saying: "Beddie-bye! Pretty bird. Beddie-bye!"

As both Girls ceremoniously release the dolls down the ramps, we see that the dolls are near-replicas of the child straddling the wings of the airplane above, but instead of a sporty outfit the dolls are only wearing what appear to be seaweed-covered inflatable arm floats that have grown together like wings. Both Girls then slump over the railing that supports the ramps.

Music: *triumphant symphonic score, increasing in volume.*

TALL MAN places his hands over his face and says: "Beep beep beep. Beep beep beep. Beep beep beep. Beep beep beep."

Tall Man, Girl in Skirt, and Short Man turn and watch as Girl in Pantsuit walks across the bottom of the stage-left screen, stretching her arms across the screen, then turns back and stares at them.

Deep Voice: The fear of being a-lone, but there are worse things.

Tall Man quickly dry-humps Girl in Skirt, who is slumped over the railing, then he stumbles away while Girl in Pantsuit walks back across the screen.

ONE LITTLE PIGGY
TWO LITTLE PIGGIES
THREE LITTLE PIGGIES
FOUR LITTLE PIGGIES
FIVE LITTLE PIGGIES

Deep Voice: Does one little pig-gy, does one little pig-gy, go to the i-dea fac-to-ry?

Voice: Dibitidoop. Eeep.

Deep Voice: Does a second little pig-gy go to the fac-tory of feel-ing? (Yes) Does a third little pig-gy cry, "Let me out ([whispers] No), let me out! Now, now!" And a fourth little pig-gy twists the door-knob, hard.

Sound cue: *echoing computer blip.*

50:24 **SCREENS – Antonio starts looking out. ANTONIO: "Tick tock, it's broken and it can't be fixed."**

Girl in Skirt and Short Man walk to either side of the boxing ring each holding a doll upside down then slowly dip their dolls in and out of black buckets.

Deep Voice: `Guess what, it really happened to me when I was a kid. I was a young person dream-ing, and I climbed out of a pit in this dream ([sings: I hear you knock-in' but you can't get in) a pit dug into the earth. And as I climbed up from the pit, and looked over the pit, there over my head was an airplane.`

Music cue: *haunting voice chant.*

Girl in Skirt awakes Tall Man, who is resting his head against the boxing ring, and hands him the doll, which he lifts into the air then slowly dips into a bucket inside the boxing ring.

Music: *solo coloratura opera voice.*

50:49 **SCREENS – WIPE TO: BICYCLE #2.**

LOOK WHAT THE UNCONSCIOUS MIND HATH WROUGHT?

51:03

LOOK WHAT THE UNCONSCIOUS MIND HATH WROUGHT? IMPOSSIBLE! THE UNCONSCIOUS MIND IS DEAD!

Tall Man and Short Man walk to the boxing ring, each holding dolls upside down by the feet. They curtly kiss the dolls' lips, then dip the dolls in and out of the black buckets that have been placed on the table/boxing ring. They then turn the dolls right-side up, hold them with both arms, and kiss them on the mouth again.

Deep Voice: Un-a-voi-da-ble.

Tall Man and Short Man retreat upstage.

Sound cue: *thump.*

Girl in Pantsuit rushes forward & around to the seated woman, lifts her veil and, while holding her shoulders and caressing her head, vigorously kisses her on the mouth, her whole body undulating.

Deep Voice: Un-avoi-da-ble.

SCREENS – MARIA: "Knock, knock, knock. The stone that rolls up the hill –"

Girl in Pantsuit turns just her head around to face the audience.

SCREENS – MARIA, continuing: "... back-wards, is called the e-vil one –"

Sound cue: *Chinese gong, electronic gurgling noise.*

Deep Voice: `But, what is it –`

51:28 **SCREENS – WIPE TO**: Diego lapping cream from a bowl.

Deep Voice: `... that in fact happened, hid-den, be-hind one's back?`

?

Sound cue: *electronic gurgling noise increasing in volume.*

Girl in Skirt and Tall Man walk to the upstage screen and slowly raise their dolls in front of the left corner of the screen, holding them there, so that the dolls, looking like identical twins, are side-by-side, facing outward.

51:44 **SCREENS – DISSOLVE TO**: Patricia, eyes closed.

51:49 **SCREENS – WIPE TO**: Patricia lounging in chair.

Deep Voice: `Au-to-ma-ti-cally real.` [Sound cue: *Chinese gong*] `The lost kiss.`

Music cue: *solo opera voice.*

Girl in Skirt and Tall Man lower their dolls, walk to the left edge of the screen, then turn in a circle and cradle their dolls.

51:54 **SCREENS – WIPE TO:** Diego licking milk from the bowl.

Deep Voice: But what is it that in fact hap-pened, hidden, be-hind one's back?

Sound cue: *Chinese gong, electronic gurgling noise increasing in volume.*

Music: *opera loop.*

Sound cue: *ringing phone.*

52:01 **SCREENS – WIPE TO:** close-up of Diego lapping milk.

52:17 **SCREENS – ROLL UP TO: TABLEAU OF "EAR."** A man sits on a table, his knees bent, his left hand resting on a black-and-white object situated between his legs. On his right side is a blond woman pointing at him with both of her hands; on his left side is a man with his left pant leg rolled up to his knee. He is gripping the ear of the man in the center & pointing at his own foot with his other hand.

Music cue: *repeating lieder.*

[flashing on & off]

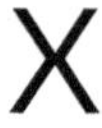

Girl in Pantsuit and Girl in Skirt walk to the Egyptian platforms and lay on them. Tall Man and Short Man hand each Girl one of the dolls, which the Girls cradle in their arms as they stare into the audience.

Deep Voice: `Sup-pose I were to pos-tu-late. Zip, be-tween this al-ways double procedure.`

Short Man and Tall Man each take a white string from out of the stage-left and stage-right walls and pulls it across the stage to between the Girls. Tall Man sits next to them then places the crown attached to the end of his string on his head. Short Man attaches his string to the crown, then places a stuffed dove on top of Tall Man's head.

TALL MAN (gravelly voice): Oh no, no, no.

53:12 **SCREENS** – **DAVID**: "Knock, knock. I immediately lost consciousness."

Deep Voice: `Here is a world, here is a world.`

Sound cue: *loud banging.*

Woman's Voice: `Here, on planet Ax-e-tron, go no fur-ther, go no fur-ther.`

Deep Voice: `Click. Click.`

Aviator enters center stage with the giant scissors, makes a cutting action, then walks off stage.

53:33 **SCREENS** – David in blindfold.

Sound cue: *chime.*

TALL MAN (gravelly voice): Ohhh no.

53:36 **SCREENS** – **DISSOLVE TO**: Patricia / Maria.

Deep Voice: `This is for you, for you on-ly.`

Short Man and Aviator each hold a giant red scissor over the legs of the Girls and snip in the air then seize the dolls from the Girls and run away.

53:52 **SCREENS – SLOW DISSOLVE TO**: Patricia laying cards.

Sound cue: *computerized distorted overlapping Russian voices.*

Girl in Skirt walks downstage while holding her hands over her eyes.

Sound cue: *chime.*

54:20 **SCREENS – ROLL UP TO: EAR.** Joe is blindfolded.

Sound cue: *ringing phone.*

Girl in Skirt grasps one of the strings connected to Tall Man's head.

54:41 **SCREENS –** DAVID: "Knock, knock. I immediately lost consciousness."

Deep Voice: `Click.`

54:48

THE ONE
THOUSAND THINGS ...

54:56

THE ONE
THOUSAND THINGS ...

THAT RULE ALL THINGS

Woman's Voice: Here, on planet [sound cue: *chime*] Ax-e-tron, no distinction is made be-tween i-deas that are good for you, and i-deas that are bad for you.

55:07 **SCREENS** – Fatima enters.

Deep Voice: Click now for ad-di-tion-al hap-pi-ness.

Short Man enters with a hammer and mocks hammering Tall Man's head twice [sound cue: *glass smashing (2x)*], then struts to stage left.

TALL MAN: Oh no.

Deep Voice: Click now for additional hap-pi-ness.

Short Man places a small porcelain doll head on top of a pirate head and mocks hammering it twice then throws the hammer to the ground.

Music cue: *haunting chant.*

Short Man raises the doll head in the air as if in an act of worship or awe and then kisses it.

SCREENS – Fatima shows her bandaged wrist, then turns her face toward the camera.

Deep Voice: The lost kiss.

Girl in Skirt and Girl in Pantsuit both spin in circles as they hold daggers above their heads, then clean the daggers with white cloths.

Music cue: *haunting horror music.*

Deep Voice (gravelly tone, emphatically): No. No. No.

Girl in Skirt and Girl in Pantsuit hold the blades to their throats.

55:44 **SCREENS — WIPE TO: EAR #2.**

Deep Voice: When the un-con-scious is dead, nothing is different ex-cept ...

SCREENS — JOE: "Knock knock. Maybe it will happen in my lifetime. Trust me. Trust me."

Music: *opera loop.*

Voice: Lamp must be re-plen-ished. Lamp must be re-plen-ished. Lamp must be re-plen-ished.

All of the actors place the different objects they are holding into the boxing ring.

56:02 Girl in Pantsuit extends her upper body into the boxing ring and holds the porcelain doll head in the air before Short Man, who holds his hand over the doll's head.

Music cue: *haunting voice.*

Deep Voice: Just like Lit-tle Red Ri-ding Hood, so mis-un-der-stood, so blind, blind, blind.

Girl in Pantsuit pulls away from Short Man & then places the doll head inside the panel of the upstage screen.

Sound cue: *chime.*

TALL MAN: No, fuck, fuck.

Deep Voice (sung): `I need noth-ing. I need noth-ing, I've ev'ry-thing I need.`

Sound cue: *chorus of haunting voices.*

Girl in Pantsuit and Girl in Skirt each retrieves a knife from the boxing ring and brings it to Tall man, who runs upstage center and mimes slitting his throat twice, once with each knife.

TALL MAN: Fuck, fuck, fuck. Fuck. No.

GIRL in Pantsuit and GIRL in Skirt (chanting in high-pitched tones as they wave white handkerchiefs): Bye-bye, bye-bye!

Deep Voice: `Oh what did I do, what did I do?`

56:48 **SCREENS – Maria removes blindfold. Joe removes blindfold. David removes blindfold.**

Girl in Pantsuit and Girl in Skirt follow Tall Man with the handkerchiefs then place them over his knives. Short Man runs to the upstage screen and opens the two panels, out of which light streams.

56:58 Tall Man stands before the edge of the upstage screen with his arms outstretched, a knife in each hand pointing upwards.

Sound cue: *computerized distorted overlapping Russian voices.*

Deep Voice: `It will nev-er hap-pen the way you want it to hap-pen.`

Short Man removes the Egyptian panels and takes them off stage.

Music cue: *violin.*

Girl in Pantsuit and Girl in Skirt carry black urns with flowers across stage and place them in the corners of the boxing ring.

57:17 **SCREENS** – blindfold back on Maria, Joe, & David.

Girl in Pantsuit and Girl in Skirt carry two more black urns with flowers to the boxing ring. Tall Man walks to the front of the boxing ring, then to downstage center, where he holds his hand over a book and points to it.

57:26 **SCREENS** – Fatima enters.

Deep Voice: Two pla-ces at once. [Sound cue: *chime.*] Two pla-ces at once.

Girl in Pantsuit and Girl in Skirt each brings another urn to the boxing ring.

Sound cue: *sirens, increasing in volume.*

Girl in Pantsuit walks to the stage-left side of the boxing ring and holds her hand over the flowers and points down at them. Girl in Skirt walks to her, places her hand on her shoulder, whispers to her.

Music cue: *opera loop.*

57:50 **SCREENS** – Fatima holds a knife over her bandaged wrist.

Sound cue: *siren decreasing in volume as if fading into the distance.*

THINGS HIDDEN SINCE . . .

Music cue: *German lieder.*

58:01

THE BEGINNING OF THE WORLD

Deep Voice (whispered): Everything here is just for you.

Sound cue: *chime.*

Bright stage lights flare on.

Deep Voice (whispered): This is for you, for you on-ly.

[flashing on & off]

X

Deep Voice: O-kay, o-kay, guess what, it really happened to me when I was a kid. I was a young person dream-ing, and I climbed out of a pit in this dream, a pit dug into the earth —.

SCREENS – JOE: "Knock knock. May-be it will hap-pen in my lifetime. Trust me. Trust me."

58:28 **SCREENS – WIPE TO: EAR #3.** The blindfolds are removed from Joe and David and then tied back on.

Sound cue: *chorus of haunting voices.*

Music cue: *Beethoven sonata.*

58:44 **SCREENS –** Fatima enters, places a knife to her bandaged wrist, holds it there.

Girl in Pantsuit, Short Man, and Girl in Skirt walk to stage right of the boxing ring and place their hands over their faces.

58:56 **SCREENS – WIPE TO CLOSE-UP OF:** Fatima's wrist with knife.

59:03 **SCREENS – WIPE TO:** Fatima's face.

Tall Man covers the Girls' heads with the white cone-hat masks while Short Man covers his own head. Each masked actor places their fingers over the eyeholes of their mask.

Deep Voice: `When the world sees it-self –`

59:09 **SCREENS – SLOW DISSOLVE TO: SAW.** Maria is splayed out on a table, a white sheet covering her body. Her arms dangle over the end of the table. A man stands over her, holding a saw against her neck. Another woman is splayed out on a table next to her & covered with red fabric.

Deep Voice: `... proof, the un-con-scious is dead.`

Sound cue: *chime, birds.*

Tall Man walks to the line-up of actors and hands each one a stuffed animal, but they do not take them from him. Tall Man watches as each lets the animal drop to the ground. Tall Man then sits downstage center facing upstage.

59:35

THINGS HIDDEN SINCE . . .

Deep Voice: `This is for you. For you on-ly.`

59:56 **SCREENS – SLOW DISSOLVE TO:** long shot of saw.

1:00:08 **SCREENS** – Joe enters with paper hat.

Tall Man stares at the upstage screen. Fatigued, he slowly raises his hand and places it against his forehead.

1:00:10 **SCREENS – WIPE TO: SAW #2.** Man tears paper open.

Deep Voice: `Click.`

Music cue: *Beethoven sonata.*

1:00:26

Sound cue: *chime.*

SCREENS – JOE: "I knew it immediately. Here it comes."

THINGS HIDDEN SINCE ... THE BEGINNING OF THE WORLD

Music cue: *violin.*

Sound cue: *chime.*

Deep Voice: This is not the world ... [sound cue: *door slamming*] but this ... is a ma-chine for ma-king the world.

Tall Man and Short Man stomp on the ground hard.

Sound cue: *door slamming (2x).*

Music cue: *Beethoven sonata.*

Sound cue: *grunting.*

Music cue: *Beethoven sonata.*

1:00:50

[flashing on & off]

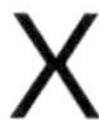

Tall Man enters with a giant newspaper-covered billboard and places it stage-left of the boxing ring.

1:01:10

Music cue: *violin.*

WHEN THE MIND IS EMPTY: "WHO GOES THERE?"

1:01:18 **SCREENS – JOE:** "Knock, knock. I knew it immediately. Here it comes."

Music cue: *short repeating violin loop.*

[flashing on & off]

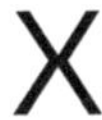

Tall Man tears the newspaper from the billboard revealing a black-&-white checkerboard; beneath it is a partially visible red-&-black checkerboard. A white X is painted across the top left corner of the billboard, which is covered with other miscellaneous images.

Tall Man takes a long black pointer with a red round tip and places it on different points on the billboard, as does Girl in Pantsuit. Tall Man then places the round red tip of his pointer against Girl in Pantsuit's head.

1:01:58 **SCREENS – DISSOLVE TO:** men falling down before the splayed-out women.

Girl in Skirt raises her pointer to the upstage screen and points it at Fatima's neck.

1:02:01 **SCREENS — WIPE TO: SAW #3.**

Sound cue: *plunking noises.*

Girl in Skirt's pointer is now resting on the upstage screen over the face of a blonde woman splayed out under a white sheet on a table.

Music cue: *modernist opera; solo baritone.*

1:02:35 **SCREENS — Joe enters. He sits, then has his head wrapped in newspaper and bound with rope.**

Deep Voice (gravelly): `Ahhh, this will make you feel bet-ter.`

Music cue: *hymns.*

Light flash.

Sound cue: *smashing plates.*

1:02:57

Deep Voice: `The fear of being a-lone, but there are, worse things.`

Sound cue: *plunking noises.*

1:03:06 Tall Man and Girl in Skirt enter anew with the pointers and place them on the upstage screen over the blond woman's face.

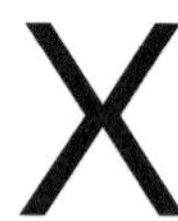

1:03:08

?

Deep Voice (with a strong emphasis on each syllable): Re-mem-ber, the truth is ne-ver a-musing. [In gravelly voice] Ne-ver spo-ken. Ac-cur-ate di-ag-no-sis.

Sound cue: *chime.*

1:03:34 **SCREENS** – hand to paper, rip. JOE: "I knew it immediately. Here it comes."

Deep Voice: Pre-ma-ture.

Sound cue: *plunking noises, smashing glass, plunking noises at louder volume.*

Four miniature parachutes drop from the ceiling and hang in the air. All actors raise their hands in the air and stare up at the parachutes then run off stage.

1:04:01 **SCREENS** – all rise and go.

Music cue: *strident violin & piano.*

Sound cue: *chime, chorus of haunting voices, plunking noises, plates smashing.*

1:04:12 **SCREENS – WIPE TO: SAW #4.** Men enter and fall.

Music: *opera loop.*

3 3 3
3 3 3
3 3 3

1:04:17 **SCREENS — WIPE TO: SAW #5.** Empty room.

Woman's Voice: Oh where, oh where is the un-con-scious [sound cue: *soft chime*] mind hiding? Oh where, oh where can it be?

Music cue: *whimsical circus-like tune under which the computerized thumping music can be heard along with the chorus of chanting voices & the machine gun noise at low volume.*

All of the actors enter carrying large diagonally-striped purple-and-yellow hinged tablets with white lace fringe, from which dangle ample bundles of black and red confetti strands. The right panel of each tablet has a golden medallion with three holes punctured into it, resembling a rudimentary face or the symbol once seen at the entrance to nuclear fallout shelters. The propeller blades of the airplane start to spin as the actors below shake the tablets back and forth in the air above their heads, then turn round and round in different directions as the stage lights quickly swell from bright to dark.

The music rises in volume and all of the actors run off stage.

1:05:17 **SCREENS — WIPE TO: SAW #6.** Men enter and fall.

Sound cue: *glass smashing.*

Voice: Dibitidoop.

Sound cue: *computerized thumping at very low volume, Chinese gong.*

1:05:31 **SCREENS — WIPE TO: SAW #7.** Men enter and fall.

Deep Voice: Click now for ad-di-tion-al hap-pi-ness.

Sound cue: *chime.*

1:05:43 **SCREENS — WIPE TO: SAW #8.** Men enter and fall.

Deep Voice: Click now for ad-di-tion-al hap-pi-ness.

Sound cue: *chime.*

SCREENS — DISSOLVE TO: people on floor.

Music cue: *swinging 20s jazz.*

Deep Voice: Click now for ad-di-tion-al hap-pi-ness.

Sound cue: *chime.*

THERE WILL BE
NO TRADITIONAL
CURTAIN CALL FOR
THIS PERFORMANCE

High-pitched Voices: BYE, BYE, BYE, BYE! BYE, BYE; GOOD-BYE!

1:06:14

THIS PERFORMANCE

IS NOW OVER

High-pitched Voices: BYE, BYE, BYE! BYE, BYE; BYE; GOOD-BYE! BYE, BYE, BYE! BYE, BYE; GOOD-BYE!

THERE WILL BE
NO TRADITIONAL
CURTAIN CALL FOR
THIS PERFORMANCE

High-pitched Voices: BYE, BYE, BYE! BYE, BYE, GOOD-BYE!

THIS PERFORMANCE

IS NOW OVER

THERE WILL BE
NO TRADITIONAL
CURTAIN CALL FOR
THIS PERFORMANCE

THIS PERFORMANCE

IS NOW OVER

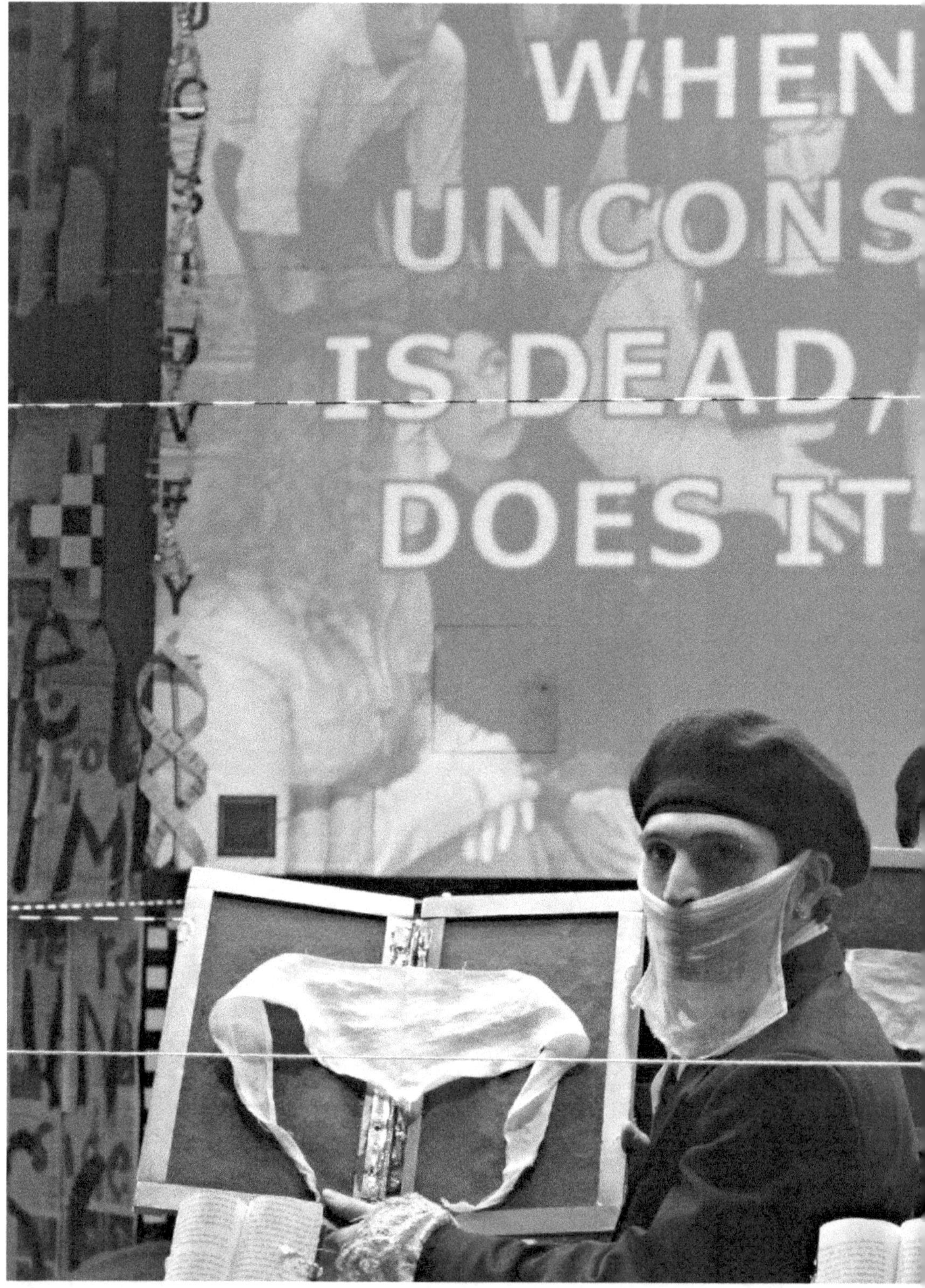
WHEN
UNCONS
IS DEAD,
DOES IT

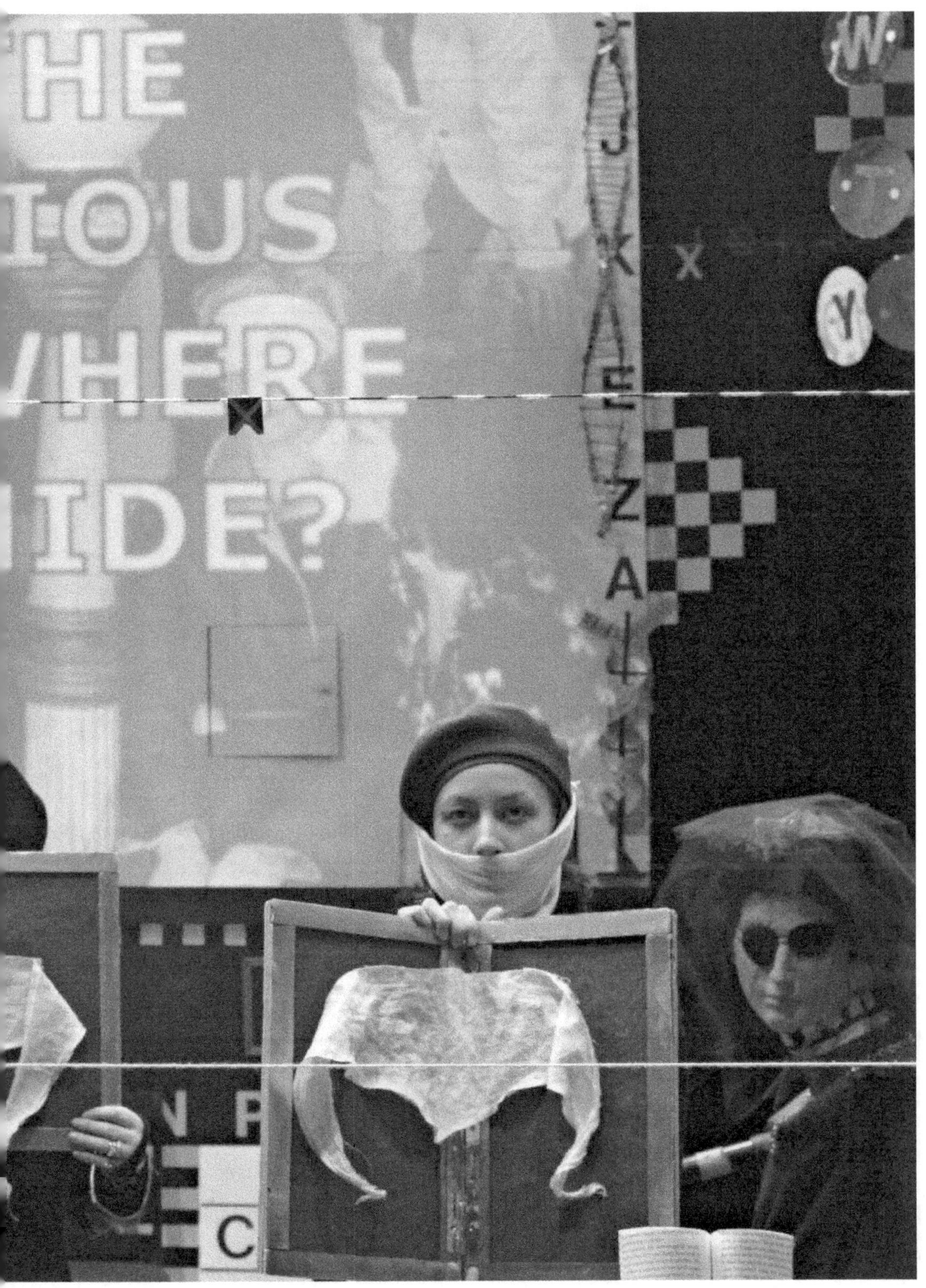
HE
IOUS
HERE
IDE?

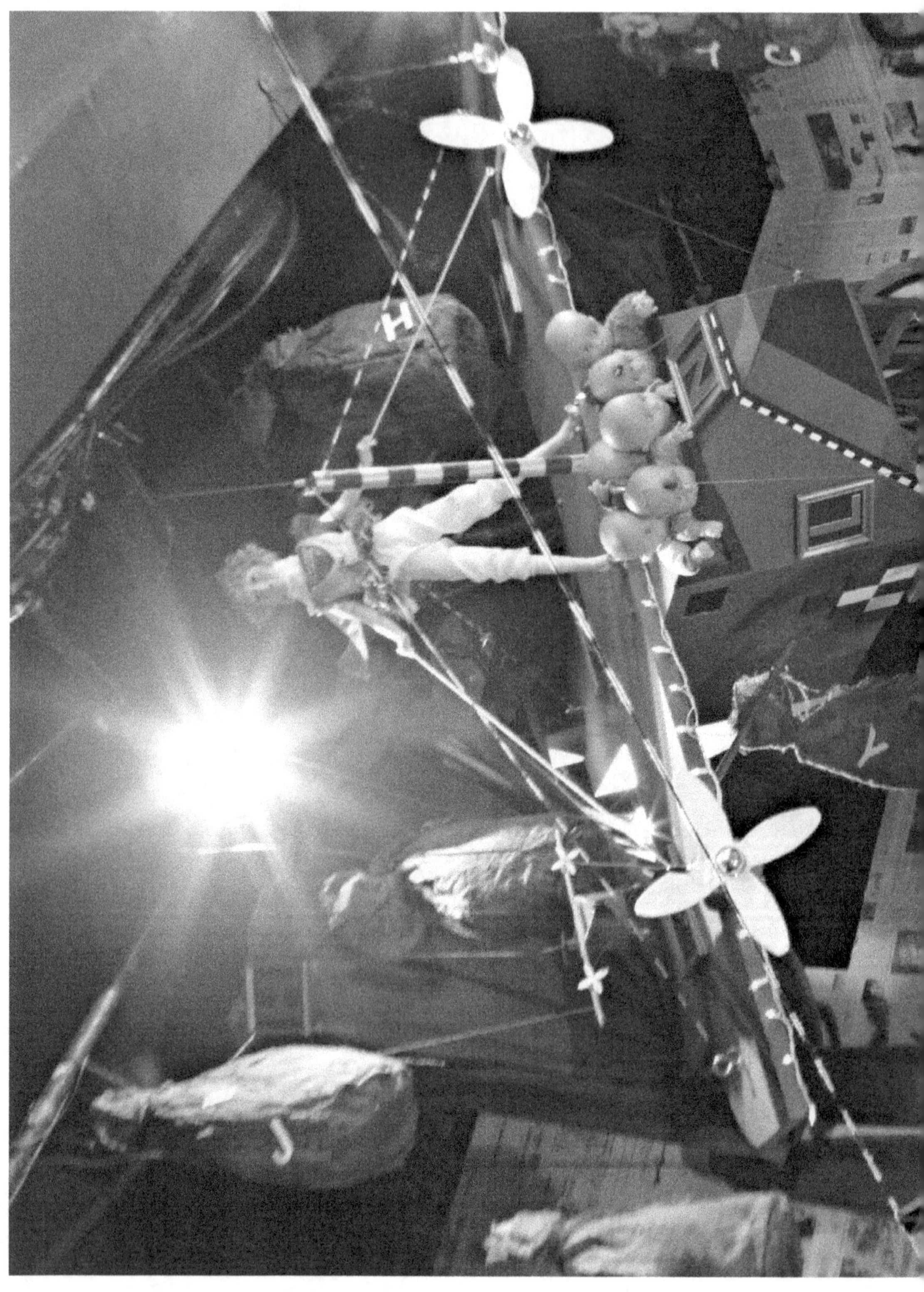

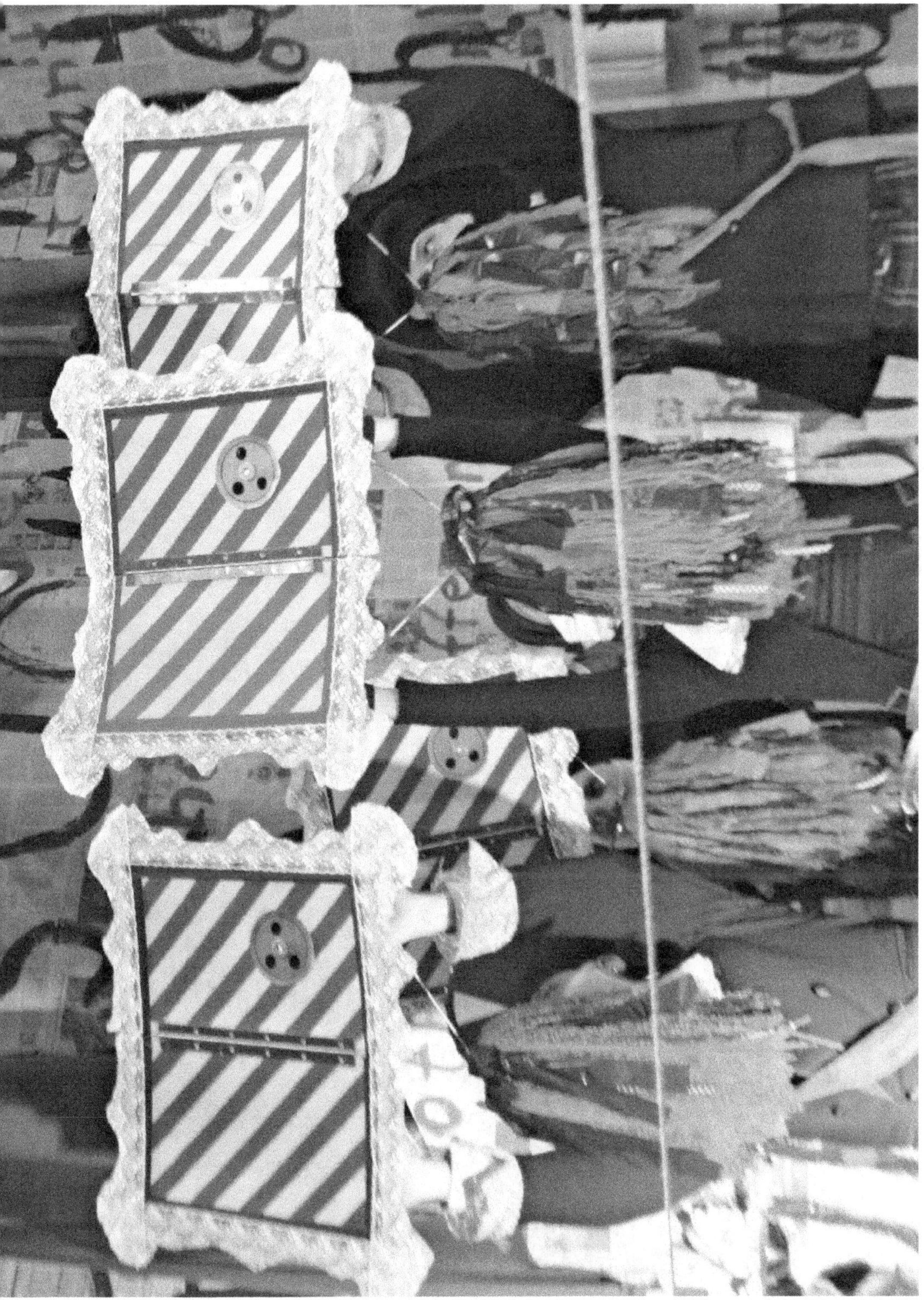

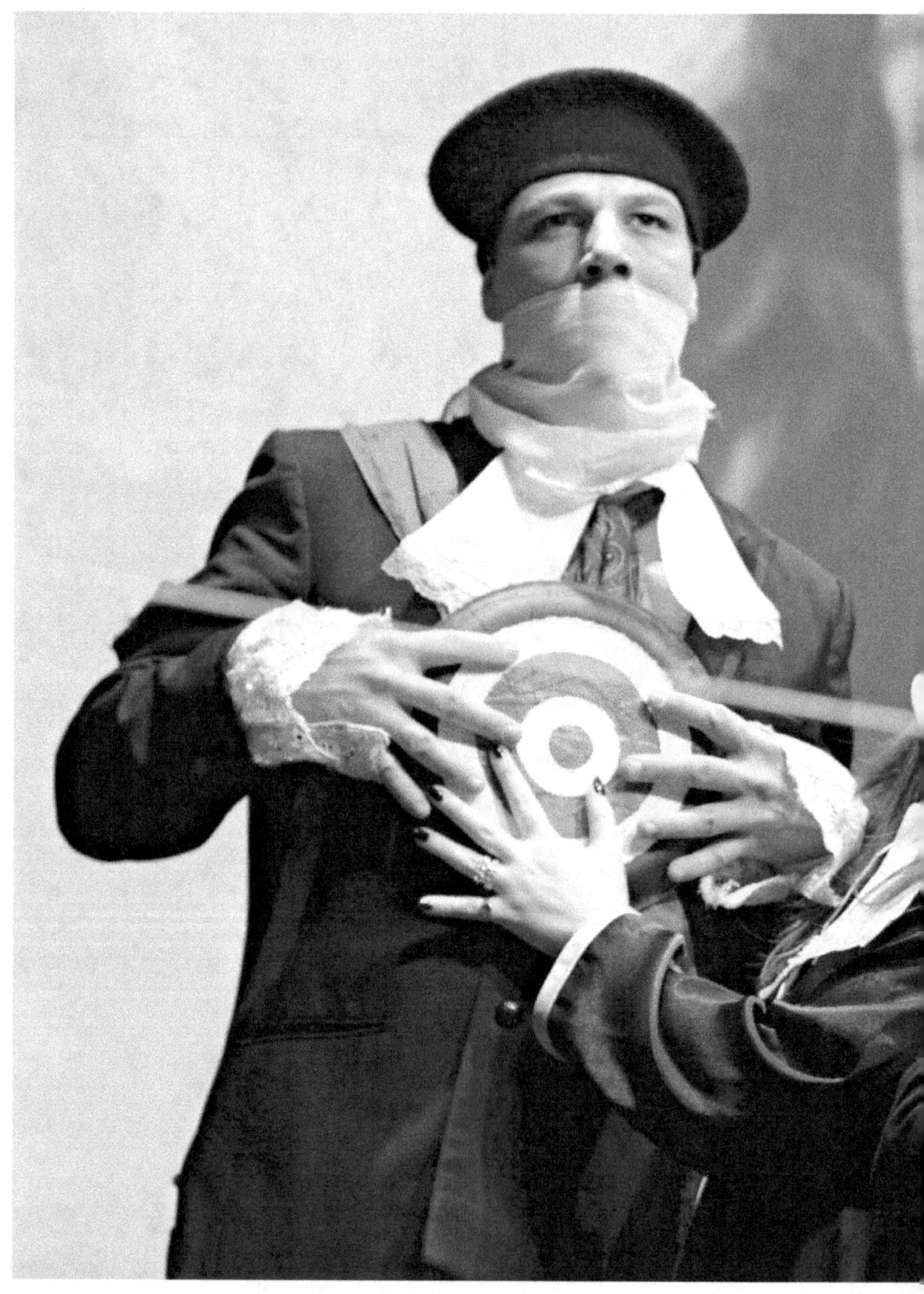

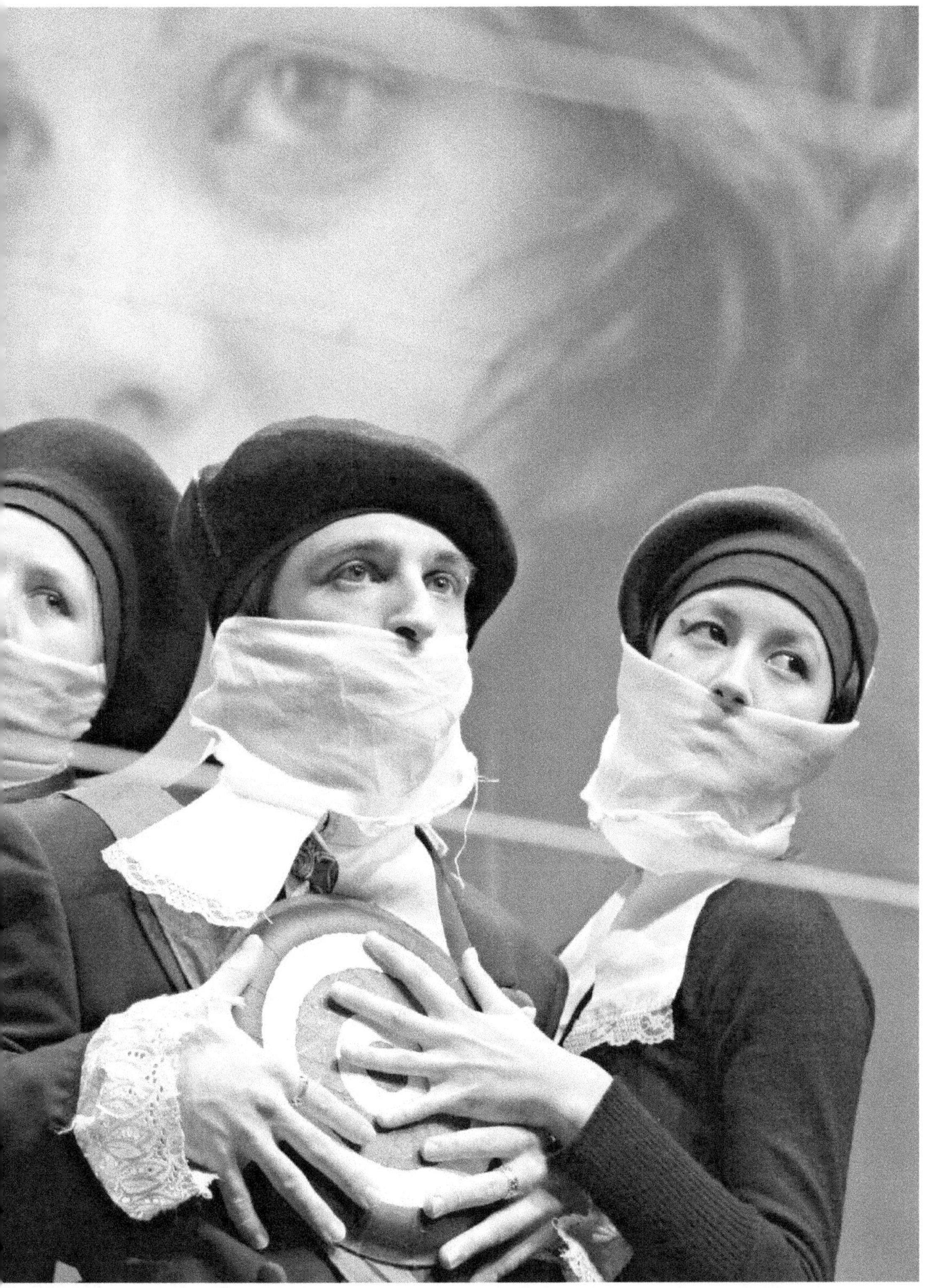

DEEP TRANCE BEHAVIOR IN POTATOLAND

(A RICHARD FOREMAN THEATER MACHINE)

PRODUCTION HISTORY

Deep Trance Behavior in Potatoland (A RICHARD FOREMAN THEATER MACHINE). Produced by the Ontological-Hysteric Theater at the Ontological at St. Mark's Theater, New York City. January 17 – April 27, 2008. Written, directed, & designed by Richard Foreman.

NYC LIVE CAST

Joel Israel: Man in Striped Suit
Caitlin McDonough-Thayer: Girl in Sailor Hat
Fulya Peker: Girl with Black Hair
Caitlin Rucker: Girl with the Golden Dress
Sarah Dahlen: Girl with the Tiara

VOICES ON TAPE

Richard Foreman, Kate Manheim, André Malraux

JAPANESE FILMED CAST & CREW

Makato Murakami
Yonki Kang
Takuya Murakawa
Ami Yamazaki
Manabu Saito
Yoshimitsu Araki
Reiko Kawashima
Fumie Takahara
Shinpei Yamada
Fumika Chiba
Dogen Sato
Fuyuko Tsuji
Mayumi Gpnda
Tamae Ando
Shirotama Hitsujiya
Junko Uchida
Tadasu Takamine
Yuya Ito
Minoru Mukouta
Hideyuki Hiraoka
Junpu Matsui
Yusuke Kimura
Ayari Itoh
Haruna Miki
Yuki Koga
Saeko Iwasaki
Yuto Kurosaka
Rie Kato
Yasuko Kurono
Nobuhiro Aragaki
Kanako Miki
Akiko Takeshita
Mariko Mori
Yumi Kobayashi
Yoko Yamamoto

ENGLISH FILMED CAST & CREW

Sinead Wall
Anthony Mamos
Dave Parkin
Hannah Nicklin
Charlie Copsey
Ryan Kerrison
Steve Middleditch
Esther Simpson
Ellie Douglas Allan
Neal Swettenham
Jo Young
Lynzi Jenkins
Amy-Louise Brassington
Jen Thorne
Anna Neil
Bex Woolston
Beth Copeland
Lydia Outhwaite
Joanna Wassall
Simon Parker

AUTHOR'S NOTE

SINCE I WAS 9 YEARS OLD –

I have been making theater.

Now, in my 70s, I increasingly find the theater a less and less appropriate arena in which to develop the laboratory-like work that obsesses me, luring me deeper and deeper into the particular truths I feel driven to explore.

What to do?

I still need the concrete, 3-dimensional arena of performance, though now admittedly semi-erased, by the slow hypnotism of tableau-based film. But the result is not just film, but rather – theater dissolving itself in the "acid-bath" of film, hopefully revealing beneath, the skeleton-support of consciousness itself. (Not theater, not film.)

This consciousness has been my 40-year obsession, as I have tried to establish an Ontological-Hysteric laboratory of the mind itself, eating away (always) at its own, (always) defective (always!) operation.

(*The 'defective' moment, is the powerhouse!*)

The stage is a large room with two projection screens on the upstage wall. Throughout the play the same film is projected on each screen. At the base of each screen is a ledge with a row of evenly distributed electric candles. Beneath the screen is a black wall with red vertical lines, like prison bars.

The stage-left and stage-right walls are lined from floor to ceiling with Victorian photographs of mediums and ectoplasmic images. Just off-center against the stage-left wall is a large black wood cabinet with glass panels; it contains numerous objects that come into use at different moments throughout the play. There are also photographs of mediums and ectoplasmic images leaning against the wall. The stage-right wall contains similar photographs in addition to two clocks. There is a large window-shaped opening in the center of the wall.

The floor is covered with a large crimson carpet. A wide white-and-black stripe runs diagonally across the carpet, left-of-center. Closer to the upstage screens are two small grand pianos, one larger and higher than the other, both of which are off-kilter, tilting toward the ground at a slight angle. To the right of the second piano is a diagonally shaped platform covered with brown carpet. Red waist-height piping runs around three-quarters of the platform. In the center of the platform is a large white cylindrical object. To the left of the platform is a black-and-gold stand with a small black flag with alchemical symbols. To the left and just in front of the first small grand piano is the same platform and object.

Two black-and-white striped strings run horizontally across the stage, and other objects, such as plastic black & white vases and books, are strewn around the stage.

Typesetting Key

00:00 (time stamp)

SCREEN – Screen tableaux

SCREEN LEGENDS

Live stage action

Voiceover

Sound & Music cue

raised-hyphen: word pronounced with elongated syllables

0:00

Deep Voice: Absent. Look.

Girl with the Golden Dress enters from stage right, stands before the upstage screen, takes a white pill from a glass bowl on the small grand piano, then turns around to face the audience. While holding up her right arm, she places the pill on her tongue, slowly retracts it, swallows the pill, then clasps her hands together in front of herself and lowers her head as if in a state of contemplation.

0:51 **SCREENS — JAPAN SCENE 1. A hallway strewn with pieces of furniture and clothing. A Japanese woman walks down the hallway. She is holding a piece of fabric in her hands, which are held behind her back, then turns toward the camera.**

Voice: hissing noise with overlapping distorted voices slowly increasing in volume.

Deep Voice: Emp-ty.

Girl with Black Hair, Girl in Sailor Hat, & Girl in Tiara all walk to stage left and stand against the wall. Girl with the Golden Dress follows them but sits against the wall. They remain still until their next action.

1:30 **SCREENS — FADE TO BLACK.**

GO TO JAPAN!

Deep Voice: Click.

1:42 **SCREENS – FADE BACK IN TO JAPAN SCENE 1.** The Japanese woman continues to slowly walk down the hallway, sometimes stopping and turning toward the camera.

Deep Voice: `Beginning. Ab-sent.`

Sound cue: *ringing phone.*

Deep Voice: `Double. One.`

2:33 **SCREENS – X-FADE TO:** close-up of feet running down the hallway.

2:46 **SCREENS – X-FADE BACK TO JAPAN SCENE 1.** The Japanese woman proceeds walking down the hallway, turns toward the camera, then walks up the staircase at the end of the hallway and out of view.

Deep Voice: `Stasis.`

3:07 **SCREENS – JAPAN SCENE 1.** A Japanese man enters in white shirt, black pants, and black hat, then turns toward the camera. Fade to black.

Deep Voice: `Look.`

Sound cue: *thunderous boom (9x).*

[The following numbers appear on screen in left-to-right order, one by one, each to a thunderous boom.]

1 2 3
4 5 6
7 8 9

10

Deep Voice: Damage.

Sound cue: *computer blip, wood block.*

3:29 **SCREENS – WIPE IN TO SHOT OF:** a Japanese woman in a floral blouse and blue skirt sitting outside on a pile of clothes. She quickly rubs her hands together again and again as if trying to clean them.

3:33 **SCREENS – FADE TO BLACK.**

11

Bulb flash.

12

3:37 **SCREENS – FADE IN TO CLOSE-UP OF:** Japanese boy & girl sitting on chairs and leaning forward.

Male Voice: He that drink-eth of this wa-ter [sound cue: *piano*] nev-er a-gain shall thirst.

JAPAN

Deep Voice: Nev-er.

3:59 **SCREENS — WIPE BACK TO:** Japanese woman in floral dress rubbing her hands together.

All of the actors remain still.

4:19 **SCREEN — X-FADE TO CLOSE-UP OF:** Japanese woman's face.

Male Voice: Jap-a-nese peo-ple of all (sta-sis) a-ges [sound cue: *thunderous wood block clack (3x)*] who understand ...

All of the actresses swiftly turn toward the audience, then slowly cover their faces with their hands & remain still.

Male Voice: O-pen this do-or. Per-ma-nent. Da-mage.

4:52 **SCREENS — FADE TO BLACK.**

MEANWHILE ON THE OTHER SIDE OF THE WORLD

Deep Voice: Real.

Music cue: *modernist piano.*

All the actresses lower their hands and turn toward the upstage screen.

5:06 **SCREENS — WIPE TO CLOSE-UP OF:** a group of English girls on a couch holding playing cards. Behind them stand other girls, their faces covered with newspaper.

Music cue: *piano.*

Male Voice: `Young En-glish peo-ple.`

All of the actresses shout in unison then turn away from the screens and cover their faces with their hands & remain still.

Deep Voice: `Work.`

5:21 **SCREENS — WIPE TO CLOSE-UP OF:** blonde English girl.

All of the actresses turn toward the screens & remain still.

Sound cue: *thunderous wood block clack (3x), computer blip.*

5:25 **SCREENS — WIPE TO CLOSE-UP OF:** shorthaired brunette English girl holding up playing cards. Another girl rearranges the cards in her hand. Wipe to the same scene again.

Male Voice: `Young En-glish peo-ple who (Look) un-der-stand` [music cue: *piano*] `... work.`

All of the actresses turn away from the screens and cover their faces.

5:40 **SCREENS — WIPE TO CLOSE-UP OF:** English women tearing paper hats from their heads, then ripping them into pieces.

All of the actresses turn toward stage right, still covering their faces.

5:44 **SCREEN — WIPE TO LONG SHOT OF:** English women ripping paper hats.

Male Voice: `Work, work ... Al-ways.`

Music cue: *solo clarinet.*

5:52 **SCREENS — WIPE TO:** two English girls in red dresses, their arms entwined. A man in a white button-up shirt sits in front of them, his hands covering his face.

Male Voice: `This is ... work. Emp-ty.`

All of the actresses remove their hands from their faces and walk to the screens, then kneel beneath them. Man in Striped Suit turns in a circle then places his hands on his chest.

6:09 **SCREENS — WIPE TO BLACK.**

Male Voice: `Go to New York Ci-ty.`

All of the actresses turn away from the screens & toward the audience and shout in unison.

Music cue: *piano.*

HE THAT
DRINKETH
OF THIS WATER
NEVER AGAIN
SHALL THIRST

Sound cue: *violent wood block clack.*

All of the actresses shout again. Man in Striped Suit turns to face the screens.

Male Voice: `Re-al.`

6:26 **SCREENS — WIPE BACK TO JAPAN SCENE 2.** A tableau of two Japanese women and a man. One woman is lying on a raised bed and the other is crouched over her like a dog. A Japanese man sits in front of them. A Japanese woman enters & removes a blindfold from the crouching Japanese woman's face.

Girl with Black Hair, Girl with the Golden Dress, and Girl with the Tiara walk to the stage-left wall. Girl in Sailor Hat kneels behind Man in Striped Suit and closes her hands over her chest as if in prayer or contemplation.

Male Voice: Click. Look.

7:01 **SCREENS — WIPE TO CLOSE-UP OF:** Japanese girl whispering in a Japanese man's ear.

Male Voice: Un-fold. A men-tal win-dow ...... (Ab-sent).
A men-tal win-dow.

7:15 **SCREENS — VERTICAL WIPE TO CLOSE-UP OF:** a room with wooden walls and lighted half-round white windows. Japanese girl in green jacket stretching her arm out in front of her. She is surrounded by a group of people, some of whom hold playing cards, face out. The girl in the green jacket extends her arm then retracts it.

Light flare on screens.

Male Voice: Hel-lo.

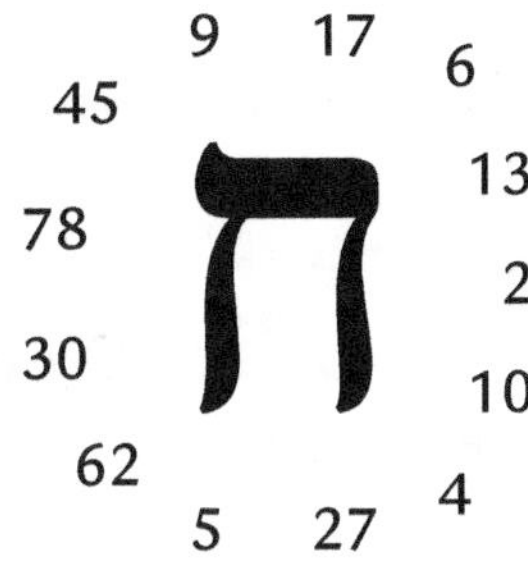

[Numbers shift clockwise (7x) to the soft *computer blip* sound cue.]

Music cue: *gentle piano refrain.*

Male Voice: Emp-ty.

7:37 **SCREENS – FADE TO:** English girl with right arm extended. She retracts her arm and extends the other.

Male Voice: Pose .... Pause.

Light flare.

7:50 **SCREENS – WIPE BACK TO JAPAN SCENE 2.**

Male Voice: Pose ... for me.

THE VISITO
R SLEEPS A
MIDST THE
EXCITEME
NT OF THE
EXPERIEN
CE THE VIS
ITOR SLEEP
S AMIDST T
HE EXCITE

Girl in Tiara, Girl in Golden Dress, and Girl with Black Hair slowly lower their hands and turn toward the screens.

Male Voice: Click.

8:05 **SCREENS – JAPAN SCENE 2.** A young girl enters and blindfolds the crouching woman. A woman in a red dress and beret whispers into the ear of a man sitting next to her.

Male Voice: `A-ware of no new (be-gin-ning) the-o-ret-i-cal ba-sis.`

Music cue: *modernist piano (3x).*

Girl in Sailor Hat walks to stage right.

8:23 **SCREENS – JAPAN SCENE 2.** The young girl enters and removes the blindfold. Japanese WOMAN: "You un-der-stand me im-me-di-ate-ly when I say..."

Stage actresses all shout in unison.

8:40 **SCREENS – JAPAN SCENE 2.** The Japanese man in front is blindfolded.

Male Voice: `He that drink-eth of this wa-ter.`

Man in Striped Suit sits beneath the stage-left screen. Girl with Black Hair stands next to him and poses, raising her hands in the air.

SCREENS – JAPAN SCENE 2. Japanese WOMAN: "Knock, knock."

In unison, Girl with the Tiara, Girl in Golden Dress, and Girl in Sailor Hat emit a high-pitched lilting moan & raise their hands in the air, striking poses.

Male Voice: `Dou-ble.`

MAN in Striped Suit: *Guarda la mia scarpa, sporca.*
Girl with Black Hair holds her hands in the air and slowly gyrates her hips.

SCREENS – Japanese **WOMAN**: "You un-der-stand me im-me-di-ate-ly when I say..."

9:11 **SCREENS – WIPE TO JAPAN SCENE 3.** A room with wooden walls & lighted half-round white windows. Against the wall is a Japanese woman in a hat holding up playing cards. To her right is the woman in the green jacket, who extends her arm toward the camera. In front of them is a group of three Japanese men sitting on the ground.

Voice: Di gi ri do, digidi doooooo, yip!

SCREENS – JAPAN SCENE 3. Japanese **WOMAN**, continuing: "... mental activity plus nobody home. [Sound cue: *thunderous boom + computer blip*] Knock, knock."

Girl with Black Hair quickly turns toward the screens, then back toward the audience while placing her right finger against her forehead.

MENTAL ACTIVITY PLUS

Male Voice: A-lert, but no new the-o-ret-i-cal ba-sis. Sta-sis.

Girl with Black Hair lowers her hand very slowly and turns toward the screens and stares at them.

Music cue: *modernist opera.*

9:36 **SCREENS – JAPAN SCENE 3.** Japanese **MAN**: "I un-der-stand you im-me-di-ate-ly when you say, I too, am al-ways in the same place. Knock, knock."

Male Voice: Beginning. Damage.

I UNDERSTAND YOU IMMEDIATE-LY WHEN YOU SAY................

9:44

I TOO AM ALWAYS IN THE SAME PLACE...............................

Girl with Black Hair walks toward the screens and reaches out to touch them, then quickly turns toward the audience, then opens the doors of the cabinet and removes a large playing card. She walks to a cylindrical ceremonial object beneath the upstage screen and holds the card over the object as she stares at the screens.

Man in Striped Suit walks to center stage, stands on a small, carpeted platform, and places his hands on his chest. Girl with the Golden Dress, Girl with the Tiara, and Girl in Sailor Hat line up next to Man in Striped Suit, then place open black books against their foreheads and slowly sway their hips back and forth while staring at Man in Striped Suit.

Music cue: *opera.*

Deep Voice: Emp-ty.

Sound cue: *loud thunderous wood block clack (3x).*

Male Voice: Nev-er.

Girl in Sailor Hat and Girl with the Tiara place their books against Man in Striped Suit's chest then place his hands over the books. They retreat to the stage-left wall. He drops the books and turns toward the screens.

10:35 **SCREEN — JAPAN SCENE 3:** Japanese WOMAN: "I un-der-stand you im-me-di-ate-ly when I say..."

A man enters and drops a white tablet into three glasses of water. The men slowly lift the glasses & stare into them.

10:52

"RESONANCE INSIDE THIS....

PERSONAL BELIEF SYSTEM"

Male Voice: `Permanent. Sta-sis.`

Man in Striped Suit walks to Girl in Sailor Hat, kneels before her, takes her hand, kisses it.

SCREEN — WOMAN (in sing-song voice): Look at you ... *Kini itte itadakeru.*

Male Voice: `Speak-ing dead, al-ways.`

Girl with the Golden Dress and Girl with the Tiara rise and walk away.

Bulb flash (2x).

Sound cue: *gentle piano refrain (3x).*

Male Voice: `Real. Da-mage.`

Sound cue: *computer blip.*

Girl with Black Hair and Girl in Sailor Hat turn toward the audience and cover their faces with their hands.

11:43 **SCREEN — JAPAN SCENE 3.** Japanese MAN: "I un-der-stand [sound cue: *thunderous wood block clack*] you im-me-di-ate-ly when you say, I too, am al-ways in the same place. Knock, knock."

Girl with Black Hair and Girl in Sailor Hat drop their hands and turn toward the screens, then toward Girl in Golden Dress and Girl with the Tiara.

Sound cue: *ringing phone.*

11:53

12

Sound cue: *ringing phone.*

Male Voice: `Ahhhhh, the con-tin-u-al. Look.`

Girl with the Golden Dress and Girl with the Tiara raise their arms and spin toward the small grand pianos, then spin away from them and back again.

12:09 **SCREENS — WIPE TO JAPAN SCENE 2.**

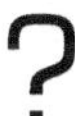

German Man (singing): *Ich ha-be dich...*

Girl with the Golden Dress and Girl with the Tiara cross their legs as they sit on the ground before the small grand pianos.

German Man (singing): *Ich ha-be dich.*

12:19

THE VISITO
R IS ALWAYS
S DEAD, AM
IDST THE E
XCITEMENT
OF THE EXP
ERIENCE TH
E VISITOR I
S ALWAYS D
EAD AMIDS
T THE EXCI
TEMENT OF

Music cue: *solo clarinet.*

Sound cue: *computerized machine-gun blast.*

Screen flare.

12:23 **SCREENS – JAPAN SCENE 2.** The crouching woman is blindfolded as a blindfold is removed from the man in the front.

Girl with Black Hair and Girl in Sailor Hat line up near the stage-left wall and shake their arms to the machine-gun blast. The Girl with the Golden Dress sits behind them and stares at the audience.

SCREENS – JAPAN SCENE 2. Japanese woman whispers in a Japanese man's ear.

Male Voice: `E-rase the frame.`

12:43 **SCREENS – WIPE TO: JAPAN SCENE 3.** The men are holding glasses against their cheeks as they stare upwards. The woman in the green jacket stands behind them & stretches her hands in front of her.

German Voice: *Ich will.*

Male Voice: The a-re-na in which no promises are made.

"ERASE THE FRAME……"

German Voice: *Ich will.*

Girl with the Golden Dress and Girl with the Tiara walk to center stage and stare at the screens. Girl with Black Hair stares at the screens from her position.

SCREENS – JAPAN SCENE 3. Japanese MAN: "I un-der-stand you im-me-di-ate-ly …"

12:59 **SCREENS – WIPE TO: JAPAN SCENE 2.**

Male Voice: Real.

SCREENS – JAPAN SCENE 3. Japanese MAN, continuing: "… when you say, I too."

Male Voice: A door o-pe-ning.

All of the actresses emit rising moans then faint in unison.

Music cue: *modernist opera.*

Male Voice: Click.

13:18 **SCREENS — JAPAN SCENE 3.** The Japanese man in front of the bed is blindfolded by a Japanese woman in a pink dress.

Male Voice: No re-la-tion-ship exists be-tween what happens on stage and what is hap-pen-ing on the il-lum-i-na-ted screen [music cue: *gentle piano*] ex-cept (Look) suddenly – CLICK, and a pro-found relationship –

Man in Striped Suit retrieves two white pieces of paper from the cabinet. There is a large question mark on each piece of paper. He sticks one on each of his shoulders then leans against the cabinet.

Woman (screaming): One, two, three, four!

Male Voice, continuing: ... does now ex-ist. Click.

Woman (screaming): One, two, three, four!

Music cue: *screeching violin at very loud pitch.*

German Man (singing): *Ich ha-be dich.*

13:45 **SCREENS — WIPE TO JAPAN SCENE 2.**

Male Voice: It's that sim-ple.

"MAKE THIS ....

MENTAL EXPERIMENT"

Male Voice: The feel-ing of no feel-ing ...... That deep feel-ing. Emp-ty.

14:09 **SCREENS — WIPE TO JAPAN SCENE 2.**

?

All of the actors line up adjacent to the stage-left wall & stare at the screens.

14:18 **SCREENS — FADE TO BLACK.**

MEANWHILE
(MEANWHILE)

Male Voice: Pause.

The actors rise and spin around, stare at the audience, then cover their faces with their hands.

14:30 **SCREENS — FADE IN TO ENGLAND SCENE 1.** A woman seated at a long table covered with open books. A man in a suit stands behind her.

Male Voice: Im-me-di-ate-ly, go to En-gland.

The actors step backwards.
Bulb flash.

Male Voice: Ho-ver-ing (Click).

14:38 **SCREENS — VERTICAL WIPE TO ENGLAND SCENE 1.** The woman at the head of the table is now face down, her arms stretched in front of her. The books are closed and before each one sits a woman with her hands folded as if in prayer.

Music cue: *hymn.*

Male Voice: Beginning.

In unison, the actors slowly remove their hands from their faces then stagger forward and lean against the stage-left wall with their hands as if fainting.

Male Voice: Young En-glish people who un-der-stand ... Double (absent) world.

The actors move off the wall and stare at the screens.

SCREENS – English GIRL: "The forgotten premise. Trust me. [Sound cue: *computer blip (2x).*] **I go backwards. Trust me. I repeat myself."**

15:25 **SCREENS – WIPE TO ENGLAND SCENE 1. The praying women sing.**

Female Voice (sung in high, cracked tone): Ear-ly. Ear-ly in the morn-ing.

The Girl with Black Hair attaches a question mark to the back of Man in Striped Suit. The women all leave. The Man in Striped Suit removes the paper question marks from his back & crumples them into balls.

1 2 3
4 5 6
7 8 9

Female Voice (sung in high, cracked tone): Ear-ly in the mor-ning.

15:36 **SCREENS – WIPE TO ENGLAND SCENE 1.** The women begin flipping through the books, swiftly turning the pages, reading in various directions.

Male Voice: Noth-ing in the heart, in the –

15:40

1 2 3
4 5 6
7 8 9

Man in Striped Suit tosses the crumpled paper question marks into the cylindrical object then faces the audience.

Male Voice, continuing: ... mind, in the be-hav-ior. Nothing in the head's busi-ness. Noth-ing in the ver-i-fi-a-ble fact, or the ver-i-fi-a-ble fu-ture.

15:59 **SCREENS** – The praying women look up & begin singing again.

Female Voice (sung in high, cracked tone): Ear-ly in the mor-ning.

German voice: *Ich will.*

THE VISITO
R SLEEPS A
MIDST THE
EXCITEME
NT OF THE
EXPERIEN
CE THE VIS
ITOR SLEEP
S AMIDST T
HE EXCITE

16:01 **SCREENS — VERTICAL WIPE TO ENGLAND SCENE 3.**

Voice (French accent): *A-mer-ica, A-mer-i-ca, we're all living in A-mer-i-ca.*

Male Voice: Sta-sis in Ja-pan. Sta-sis in En-gland.

Girl with the Tiara, Girl with the Golden Dress, & Girl with Black Hair walk onstage with black plastic vases with plastic flowers.

Male Voice: Ahhhhh, that thing.

Voice (French accent): *A-mer-ica, A-mer-i-ca, we're all living in A-mer-i-ca.*

Sound cue: *thunderous boom.*

Man in Striped Suit bumps into Girl with Black Hair from behind, then falls to his knees then to the ground, fainting.

Female Voice: I remember!

Male Voice: That thing. Sta-sis.

An enormous hummingbird enters from stage right and slowly rocks back and forth behind the small grand piano. The actresses retreat to stage left.

Voice: *Votre imagination vous transporterez au pays de la vérité, et vous n'aurez plus à réflechir à tant de ces choses.*

Voice (French accent): *A-mer-ica, A-mer-i-ca, we're all living in A-mer-i-ca.*

Male Voice: Ho-ver-ing.

SCREENS – Japanese BOY: "You understand me immediately when I say this real speaking, i.e., what, not what."

Male Voice: Why now? May-be now?

Sound cue: *siren.*

The actresses all point toward the giant hummingbird while staring at the audience.

Male Voice: Why now? May-be now? Double.

Voices: Ah, ah, ah, ah, ah.

Male Voice: Don't look. Go to o-ther worlds. Never.

Sound cue: *chime.*

Girl with the Golden Dress, Girl with Black Hair, and Girl with the Tiara slowly creep toward center stage.

Voice: Fuuum!

Male Voice (sung): Me and my sha-dow.

SCREENS – Japanese BOY: "You un-der-stand me im-me-di-ate-ly when I say –"

17:19 **SCREENS – WIPE TO: JAPAN SCENE 2. Two Japanese men are seated against the back wall holding violins. A third Japanese man is comforting a Japanese woman seated next to him.**

1 2 3
4 5 6
7 8 9

Music cue: *modernist piano refrain.*

Male Voice: `Sta-sis.`

Female Voice (sung in high, cracked tone): `Ear-ly in the mor-ning. Ear-ly in the mor-ning. Ear-ly in the mor-ning.`

Male Voice: `Permanent.`

Sound cue: *computer blip.*

Girl with Black Hair walks to the small grand piano, takes a white pill from a glass bowl, holds it up to the audience, places it on her tongue, then very slowly retracts her tongue and swallows the pill.

Bulb flash.

Music cue: *modernist piano.*

Girl with Black Hair sits next to the small grand piano, crosses her legs, places her hands on her knees, stares into the audience.

Male Voice: `Dou-ble (real) world.`

Girl in Sailor Hat enters, walks to stage right, tosses a crumpled piece of fabric into the cylindrical object, then sits behind Girl with Black Hair and begins rubbing her hands together.

Girl with the Golden Dress and Girl with the Tiara walk to the edge of the screens and stare at them. Girl with Black Hair rises and stands behind her, then stares up at the screens, covers her ears and screams.

SCREENS – Japanese GIRL: "I understand you immediately, when I say: tick, tock."

18:29

\+ + + +

\+ + + +

\+ + + +

X X X X

X X X X

X X X X

SCREENS – JAPAN SCENE 3. Japanese GIRL: "I am here; tick, tock. Proof. Tick, tock."

Male Voice: Look.

Girl in Sailor Hat rises and moves to the screens.

\+ + + +

\+ + + +

\+ + + +

SCREENS – JAPAN SCENE 3. The Japanese men raise the violins above their heads.

18:51 **SCREENS – WIPE TO JAPAN SCENE 4.** Four blindfolded women sit at the edge of a piano with sheet music in their hands. A Japanese man is sprawled across the top of the piano. The face of the woman sitting behind the piano is covered by the hands of another Japanese woman.

X X X X

X X X X

X X X X

18:58

+ + + +

+ + + +

+ + + +

19:04

X X X X

X X X X

X X X X

19:12

+ + + +

+ + + +

+ + + +

Music cue: *violins.*

Male Voice: Emp-ty.

Sound cue: *sirens.*

Chorus: Ah, ah, ah, ah, ah.

Girl in Black Hair removes her hands from her head. She watches the Man in Striped Suit slowly rise from the ground, then approaches the screens.

Sound cue: *thunderous boom.*

Female Voice (sung in high, cracked tone): Ear-ly in the mor-ning.

Voice (woman with Japanese accent): Look at you. *Kini itte itadakeru*?

Male Voice: Don't look.

Man in Striped Suit (slapping head): *Molta gente giapponese.*

Sound cue: *siren.*

Male Voice: Point ...

Music cue: *solo opera voice.*

19:42 **SCREENS — WIPE TO JAPAN SCENE 3.**

"A WORLD THAT RIVALS.....

..........THE REAL WORLD"

Male Voice, continuing: ... of con-cen-tra-tion. Click.

20:03 **SCREENS — SLOW WIPE TO CLOSE-UP OF: Japanese man and girl. The three Japanese men crawl forward on their knees then raise their violins above their heads as they stare at the Japanese girl.**

Male Voice: Look.

Man in Striped Suit circles the stage then stands behind a bound scroll. He holds his hands together as if in prayer before the object.

Male Voice: Sha-ken by things. Ab-sent.

20:09 **SCREENS — X-FADE TO CLOSE-UP OF: Japanese woman in floral dress rubbing her hands.**

Girl with the Golden Dress, Girl in Sailor Hat, & Girl with the Tiara approach Man in Striped Suit and hold open black books up to his head and shake them back and forth as the Girl with Black Hair stands in front of them and stares at the audience while holding her book on her chest.

20:35 **SCREENS — WIPE TO BLACK.**

Girl with the Golden Dress, Girl in Sailor Hat, and Girl with the Tiara slam their books closed. The latter two hand their books to the Girl with the Golden Dress and walk away.

Male Voice: Emp-ty.

Music cue: *gentle piano refrain.*

MEANWHILE ADDITIONAL YOUNG ENGLISH PEOPLE

GIRL with Black Hair: *Teşekkür ederim,* which means, 'Thank you, ver-y much.'

Girl with the Golden Dress approaches Girl with Black Hair & takes the book from her, then walks away.

Male Voice: Pause.

20:53 **SCREENS – FADE IN TO ENGLAND SCENE 2.** A library. Groups of men and women clustered together, some crouching, some sitting. Two girls place their fingers on the face of a blonde haired woman holding a book against her chest. A black haired woman wraps her arms around a kneeling man.

SCREENS – English MAN: "The forgotten premise. Trust me; trust me; trust me."

Girl with Black Hair walks to the Man in Striped Suit and raises a wooden sword above his head. He lowers his head onto the bound scroll and she places the sword on the back of his neck.

? ? ? ? ? ? ? ? ? ? ? ?

Male Voice: Click. Like speak-ing dead.

Girl with Black Hair pretends slicing off the head of Man in Striped Suit while making a slicing sound with her lips then turns towards the screens and raises the sword above her head.

German Voice: *Ein klein-er Mensch.*

20:53

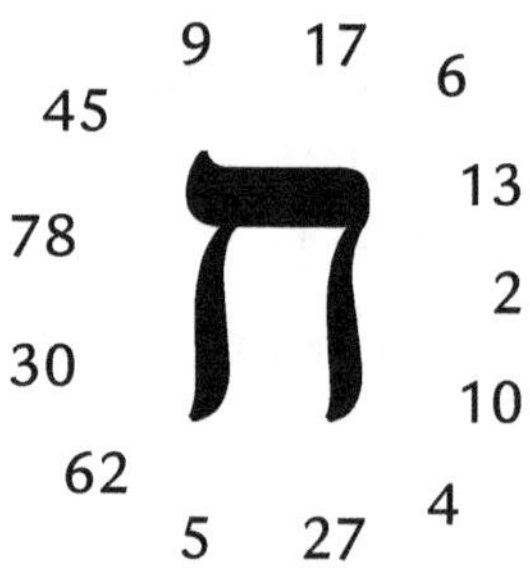

[sequence shifts six times (the numbers moving clockwise) to *computer blip* sound cue]

21:32 **SCREENS – WIPE TO ENGLAND SCENE 2.** The people in the background cover the crouching man and woman with a white sheet. **X-FADE** to the same scene as a group of blonde women slowly crouch toward the covered bodies.

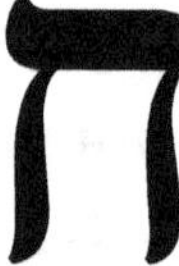

Male Voice: Ab-sent.

21:47 **SCREENS – X-FADE TO CLOSE-UP OF:** a blindfolded man in a suit with his pants rolled up to his knees. He is sitting on a table covered with red velvet. Between his legs is a stack of books; he places his hands on them.

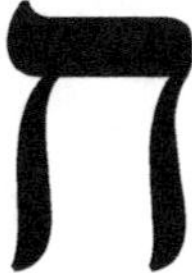

SCREENS – Japanese WOMAN: "Tick, tock."

21:53 **SCREENS – WIPE TO JAPAN SCENE 4.**

Male Voice (elongating each syllable): Dou-ble world.

Music cue: *strident violin/piano, solo clarinet.*

SCREENS – Young Japanese MAN: "I un-der-stand you im-me-di-ate-ly, when I say I am being im-pul-sive by choice. Tick, tock."

THE VISITO
R IS ALWAY
S DEAD, AM
IDST THE E
XCTEMENT
OF THE EXP
ERIENCE TH
E VISITOR I
S ALWAYS D
EAD AMIDS
T THE EXCI
TEMENT OF

French Voice: ... *où nous écoute* ...

Male Voice (elongating each syllable): Ho-ver-ing.

22:24 **SCREENS — WIPE TO JAPAN SCENE 4.** The other people exit the room, leaving alone the man with the books.

?

22:28 **SCREENS — WIPE TO JAPAN SCENE 4.**

Music cue: *circus music, opera.*

Male Voice: `Sta-sis.`

22:40 **SCREENS — WIPE TO:** room with a table covered with a white tablecloth.

Male Voice: `False gods al-ways.`

Music cue: *opera.*

22:44 **SCREENS — WIPE TO:** room with table and chair.

Male Voice: `Be-gin-ning.`

Man in Striped Suit turns around & faces the upstage screen. Girl with Black Hair stands behind him and places the sword against the back of his neck.

22:50 **SCREENS — FADE TO BLACK.**

THE IDENTICALLY NAMED MOMENT

Male Voice: `Im-me-di-ate-ly, go (Damage) to o-ther worlds.`

23:06 **SCREENS – WIPE TO JAPAN SCENE 5.** A woman wearing a green dress and white gloves is stretched across the table. Seated next to her is a woman in a black dress; behind her stands a man covering her eyes with his hands.

Sound cue: *thunderous boom (3x).*

Voice: `Di gi ri do, digidi doooooo, yip!`

Girl with the Golden Dress enters, walks to center stage, then drops to her knees beside the small grand piano & places her hands on the keys.

Male Voice: `Dou-ble.`

23:22

"ENTERING SOON THE ROOM ....

.... OF INTENSE LIGHT"

Girl in Sailor Hat drops a sledgehammer on the ground, then falls over, stretching her hands to her feet.

Male Voice: `Never.`

Music cue: *ballroom piano.*

23:33 **SCREENS – WIPE TO JAPAN SCENE X.** A Japanese girl in a green dress & black boots is crouched on top of a table; behind her is a Japanese woman. A Japanese man is standing next to her. He gazes at her, then turns to face the camera.

Music cue: *solo clarinet.*

Female Voice (sung): `Ear-ly in the mor-ning. Ear-ly in the morn-ing. Early in the mor-ning.`

> **SCREENS — JAPAN SCENE X.** Japanese WOMAN: "I un-der-stand you im-me-di-ate-ly when you say this im-pulse is now dou-ble im-pulse."

Woman (screaming): `One, two, three, four!`

Male Voice: `Sta-sis.`

Sound cue: *ringing phone.*

Woman (screaming): `One, two, three, four!`

> **SCREENS — JAPAN SCENE X.** Japanese WOMAN: "One, two, three, four. One, two, three, four."

24:01

1 2 3
4 5 6
7 8 9

Music cue: *violin/piano at violent pitch.*

> The Hummingbird enters & stretches its beak toward Girl in Sailor Hat as if to eat of her body.

24:05 **SCREENS — WIPE TO JAPAN SCENE 5.** A room in the day-time. Two Japanese men are sitting on a couch; one of them is sleeping; next to the other, there is a pile of several female dolls; behind the couch is a Japanese man in a blindfold. His arms are folded across his chest.

French singing: *We're all living in A-mer-i-ca!*

Music cue: *solo clarinet, triumphant marching band music.*

Man in Striped Suit crosses to the small grand piano & takes Girl in Sailor Hat by the hand and escorts her away from the piano. He walks with her to the stage-left wall. They both place their hands over their faces, then stretch out their arms to lean against the ectoplasmic pictures.

Girl with the Tiara walks to an upstage screen & places her hands against it. She stares at the screen in awe.

SCREENS – Young Japanese MAN: "You understand me now, when I say this real system. Knock, knock. I do not name this system."

Woman (screaming): 1, 2, 3, 4. 1, 2, 3, 4.

Sound cue: *nuclear alarm, war siren, marching band music increases in volume and intensity.*

Man in Striped Suit walks to center stage, picks up the wooden sword, examines it, then thrusts it into the cylindrical object to his left.

25:15

"MAKING THE TRUTH ....

.... SINGLE ALWAYS"

Girl with Black Hair takes a white pill from the glass bowl on the small grand piano and displays it to Man in Striped Suit. Girl with the Golden Dress and Girl with the Tiara turn toward the upstage screen & cover their faces with their hands.

Sound cue: *loud wood block clack.*

Woman (screaming): 1, 2, 3, 4. 1, 2, 3, 4.

Girl with Black Hair places the pill on her tongue then very slowly retracts it. She raises her hands in front of her face. Man in Striped Suit kneels and bows before the cylindrical object.

Sound cue: *nuclear alarm.*

25:28

+ + + +
+ + + +
+ + + +

Sound cue: *nuclear alarm (2x).*

25:36

X X X X
X X X X
X X X X

25:44

+ + + +
+ + + +
+ + + +

Sound cue: *war siren, nuclear alarm (7x).*

Girl with Black Hair turns toward the screens & covers her face with her hands.

25:58

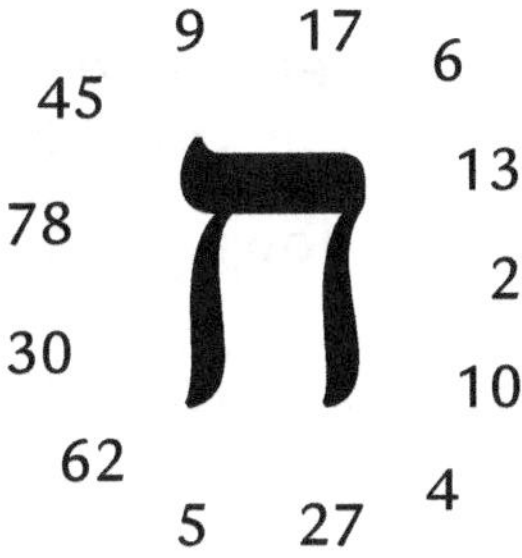

[sequence shifts six times (the numbers moving clockwise) to *computer blip* sound cue]

Girl with the Golden Dress and Girl with the Tiara open their hands, turn toward the audience, then back toward the screens.

26:05 **SCREENS — JAPAN SCENE X. The Japanese man moves behind the Japanese woman & covers her eyes with his hands.**

Sound cue: *war siren.*

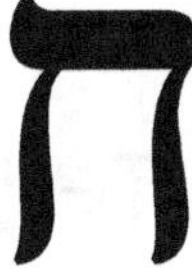

Man in Striped Suit faints and falls backwards.

26:22

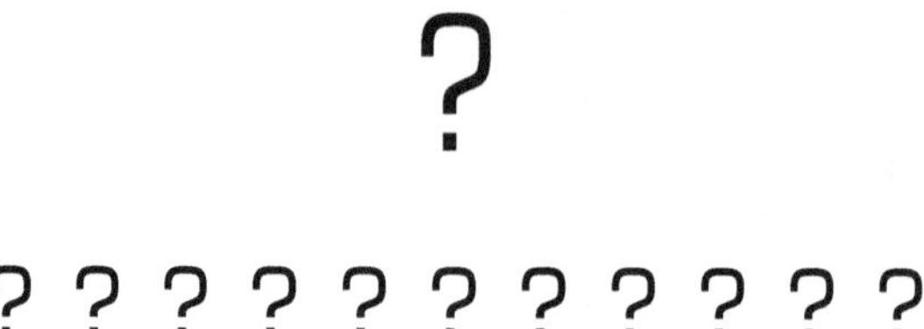

SCREENS – JAPAN SCENE X. A Japanese woman enters with a shopping cart full of stuffed animals. She is only visible from the neck down.

Man in Striped Suit tries to rise, but faints again, falling forwards.

Sound cue: *thunderous boom (3x).*

26:36

? ? ? ? ? ? ? ? ? ? ?

SCREENS – JAPAN SCENE X. The Japanese woman lowers her head into view and turns toward the camera.

Girl with the Tiara has two ritual wands with bells & holds them over Man in Striped Suit.

26:57

Music: *marching band tune ends.*

"MAKING THE TRUTH ....

.... SINGLE ALWAYS"

27:07 **SCREENS – WIPE TO: JAPAN SCENE 5.** The man covers the woman's eyes with his hands.

Male Voice: `Emp-ty.`

Girl with the Tiara turns toward the screens and shakes the wands at them.

SCREENS – JAPAN SCENE 5. The Japanese woman enters from the left, wheeling in a bicycle. The basket is full of stuffed animals.

Girl with the Tiara shakes the wands at the screen again and again.

Male Voice: `O-pen this do-or.`

Female Voice (sung in high, cracked tone): `Ear-ly in the mor-ning.`

Male Voice: `O-kay.`

Female Voice (sung in high, cracked tone): `Ear-ly in the mor-ning.`

Male Voice: `Ahhhhhh.`

Music cue: *discordant violins at extreme pitch.*

27:44 **SCREENS – WIPE TO: JAPAN SCENE 5.** Now, only the two men are on the couch. Behind them is a Japanese woman. She removes a blindfold from her eyes, then walks away. Young Japanese MAN: "You un-der-stand me now when I say, this world sys-tem: knock, knock. I do not name this sys-tem."

Male Voice: `Be-gin-ning.`

SCREENS – JAPAN SCENE 5. A Japanese man enters, kneels behind the couch, blindfolds himself, then crosses his arms over his chest.

German Voice: *Ich will ... Ich will.*

28:05 **SCREENS – WIPE TO: JAPAN SCENE X.** The woman on the bicycle stares into the camera.

German voice: *Ich will. Ich will.*

THE VISITO
R IS ALWAY
S DEAD, AM
IDST THE E
XCTEMENT
OF THE EXP
ERIENCE TH
E VISITOR I
S ALWAYS D
EAD AMIDS
T THE EXCI
TEMENT OF

Man in Striped Suit rises from the ground, rips a paper question mark from his back, crumples it and throws it into the cylindrical object.

Sound cue: *computer blip.*

Girl with the Golden Dress, Girl with the Tiara, and Girl with Black Hair enter together with a carpet. Girl with Black Hair kneels before the small grand piano &

stares back at the audience. Girl with the Golden Dress and Girl with the Tiara wrap the carpet around Man in Striped Suit's legs.

Woman (screaming): `1, 2, 3, 4!`

28:19 **SCREENS – WIPE TO: JAPAN SCENE 5.**

German Voice: *Ein klein-er Mensch.*

Girl with the Golden Dress kneels over the small grand piano and stares at the audience. Girl in Sailor Hat kneels between Girl with the Golden Dress & Girl with the Tiara, bends down, then walks off stage. Girl with the Tiara waves to the audience, then grabs hold of a striped pole and, along with the Girl with the Golden Dress, lifts it into the air.

Woman (screaming): `1, 2, 3, 4! 1, 2, 3, 4!`

Male Voice: `Double.`

Girl with Black Hair removes the carpet from Man in Striped Suit's legs & walks away from him then holds the carpet up like a toreador's cape.

Music: *solo clarinet.*

Sound cue: *hissing noise with overlapping distorted voices slowly increasing in volume.*

SCREENS – Japanese WOMAN: "I understand you im-me-di-ate-ly when you say this impulse is now double impulse. One, two, three, four. One, two, three, four."

Man in Striped Suit bends down like a bull, forming horns with his hands.

28:58 **SCREENS — WIPE TO: JAPAN SCENE 5.**

Sound cue: *thunderous boom (3x).*

1 2 3
4 5 6
7 8 9

Male Voice: Sta-sis.

Sound cue: *thunderous boom.*

29:08

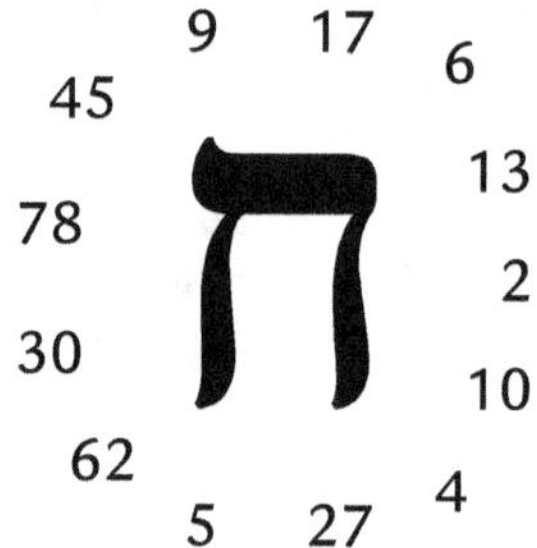

[sequence shifts six times (the numbers moving clockwise) to *computer blip* sound cue]

Man in Striped Suit enters with a floral head-cage, walks to center stage, then places it on his head. Girl in Sailor Hat lies over a stool in front of the stage-right small grand piano and places her hands on the ground in front of her. Man in Striped Suit removes the head-cage and walks offstage.

Sound cue: *hissing noise with overlapping distorted voices slowly increasing in volume.*

Male Voice: Here it is. Ok. Be-gin-ning. (One) Go to o-ther worlds, immediately.

29:37 **SCREEN — FADE TO BLACK.**

Deep Voice: One.

1

29:39

GO TO JAPAN

SCREEN — FADE-IN. Japanese **VOICE**: "Look at you. *Kini itte itadakeru*?"

Male Voice: Look. Look.

29:49 **SCREENS — FADE TO BLACK.**

2

SCREENS — Japanese **VOICE**: "Look at you. *Kini itte itadakeru*? Look at me."

Deep Voice: Look.

29:54 **SCREENS — FADE TO: JAPAN SCENE.**

GO TO
ENGLAND

Male Voice: Aware.

29:56 **SCREENS — FADE TO BLACK.**

3

29:59 **SCREENS — FADE TO JAPAN.**

GO TO
NEW YORK
CITY

30:02 Girl with the Golden Dress and Man in Striped Suit rise & stare at the screens.

63 28 17

91 32 54

44 76 83

Man in Striped Suit points at the screens, then turns to the audience. Girl with Black Hair stares at the audience.

30:15 **SCREENS — WIPE TO: JAPAN SCENE 5.** Everyone exits.

Sound cue: *hissing noise with overlapping distorted voices slowly increasing in volume.*

30:26 **SCREENS — WIPE TO: JAPAN**, couch scene: two Japanese men rise from the couch and leave.

Male Voice: `Open this door. Sta-sis.`

30:36 **SCREENS — WIPE TO:** room with table and chair.

Male Voice (sung, with a strong emphasis on each syllable): `Me and my sha-dow.`

MAN in Striped Suit (imitating, and slapping his hand on his forehead): "Me & my sha-dow."

German Voice: *Ich will.*

30:45

ENGLISH PEOPLE ARE AFRAID

Male Voice (sung, lyrically): `Me and my sha-dow.`

30:48 **SCREEN — WIPE TO: ENGLAND SCENE 4.** A long wood table in a gallery before which stand a group of women holding their hands on the sides of their faces, like horse-blinders.

Music cue: *solo jazz piano.*

Male Voice: Da-mage.

Music cue: *solo clarinet.*

Male Voice: Real.

31:04 **SCREENS — WIPE TO: ENGLAND SCENE 4.** A girl enters with yellow scarf and eye-patch. English **WOMAN**: "Care-ful, care-ful."

Girl with Black Hair covers Girl in Sailor Hat with the fabric then places her hands over her body.

31:19 **SCREENS — WIPE TO: ENGLAND SCENE 4.** A man in a white shirt and tie enters and holds the eye-patch woman from behind.

French Voice (reciting): *Ceux qui nous écoute ...*

Girl with Black Hair stares at the audience while resting her hands on the covered body.

Sound cue: *hissing noise with overlapping distorted voices slowly increasing in volume.*

Deep Voice: Stop. Never.

Sound cue: *computerized machine-gun blast repeating endlessly.*

SCREENS — ENGLAND SCENE 5. A bicycle is slowly pulled across a raised platform by the woman with the eye-patch and a woman in a black dress.

31:45 **SCREENS — WIPE TO:** English girls covering their faces with their hands and opening and closing their hands.

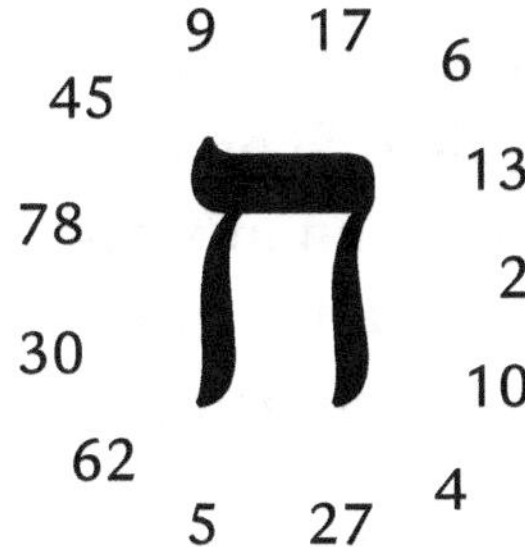

[sequence shifts six times (the numbers moving clockwise) to *computer blip* sound cue]

31:54 **SCREENS – X-FADE TO CLOSE-UP OF:** English girls.

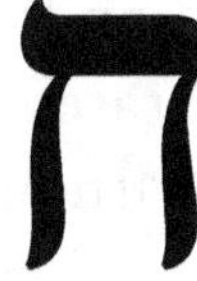

Sound cue: *thunderous computerized machine-gun blast continues.*

32:01 **SCREENS – WIPE TO CLOSE-UP OF:** English girl with eye patch and English man.

Girl with Black Hair removes the fabric from Girl in Sailor Hat, quickly rises, and stares at the screens.

32:20 **SCREENS – X-FADE TO CLOSE-UP OF WINDOW.**

Girl with the Tiara lies on the ground and covers herself with one of the ectoplasmic photographs. Girl with Black Hair does the same.

Voice: `faintly audible speech of distressed French woman.`

32:29 **SCREENS – WIPE UP TO: JAPAN SCENE 6.** A stairway with a brightly lit window at the top. A group of people are lined up against the wall, one on each step. At the bottom of the stairs there is a woman in a black dress sitting down and covering her eyes with her hands; next to her is a woman in a pink dress crouching before a plush floral chair.

Sound cue: *war siren.*

Woman (screaming): 1, 2, 3, 4. 1, 2, 3, 4.

Voice: speech of distressed French woman continues, volume rising.

Girl in Sailor Hat moves next to Girl with the Tiara. She kneels on the ground and rests an ectoplasmic photograph before her and stares into it. Girl with the Golden Dress covers her eyes with one hand while extending her other arm out in front of her.

Sound cue: *ringing phone.*

ONLY BEING
A TOURIST
CAN ONE
EXPERIENCE
A PLACE

Bulb flash.

Man in Striped Suit walks downstage, then turns toward Girl with the Golden Dress and holds his hands before his face as if framing the space. Girl with the Golden Dress faints.

Male Voice: `Look.`

Girl with the Tiara, Girl in Sailor Hat, and Girl with Black Hair rise from the ground with the ectoplasmic photographs and walk to the other side of the stage.

Sound cue: *war siren.*

33:21 **SCREENS – WIPE TO: JAPAN SCENE 6. Everyone, save for the woman in black, walks up the staircase.**

Girl with the Tiara, Girl in Sailor Hat, and Girl with Black Hair sit near the stage-right small grand piano and rest the ectoplasmic photographs on the ground and hide behind them. They reach over their photographs and point at them.

MAN in Striped Suit (sung in growling voice): "Me & my sha-dow."

Sound cue: *war siren.*

33:36 **SCREENS – WIPE TO CLOSE-UP OF: Japanese girl in hat, crying.**

Male Voice: `Me and my sha-dow.`

Sound cue: *thunderous wood block clack (3x).*

Music cue: *melancholic passage from Mihály Vig's score to Béla Tarr's* Werckmeister Harmóniák.

Voice: `French track continues.`

Sound cue: *war siren, thunderous wood block clack (3x).*

Light flares from behind the center of the screens.

34:12 **SCREENS — X-FADE TO: JAPAN SCENE 6.** A group of Japanese people lined up against the wall, one standing on each step of the staircase. At the foot of the staircase are two chairs upon which sit Japanese women. In front of the chairs is a blindfolded Japanese man.

34:23

? ? ? ? ? ? ? ? ? ? ?

Light flare on screen.

Girl with the Golden Dress faints.

MAN in Striped Suit (shouting): No!

34:43

NO!

? ? ? ? ? ? ? ? ? ? ?

34:44

? ? ? ? ? ? ? ? ? ? ?

MAN in Striped Suit (shouting): No! No!

NO!

? ? ? ? ? ? ? ? ? ? ?

MAN in Striped Suit: No! Beau-ti-ful la-dy!

34:51

63	28	17
91	32	54
44	76	83

83	63	28
32	54	17
91	44	76

34:53

? ? ? ? ? ? ? ? ? ? ?

34:54

76	83	63
54	17	28
32	91	44

44	76	83
17	28	63
54	32	91

34:55

? ? ? ? ? ? ? ? ? ? ?

34:56

91 44 76
28 63 83
17 54 32

32 91 44
63 83 76
28 17 54

34:57

? ? ? ? ? ? ? ? ? ? ?

34:58

54 32 91
83 76 44
63 28 17

17 54 32
76 44 91
83 63 28

34:59

? ? ? ? ? ? ? ? ? ? ?

34:56

28 17 54
44 91 32
76 83 63

63 28 17
91 32 54
44 76 83

35:01

? ? ? ? ? ? ? ? ? ? ?

35:02

Man in Striped Suit helps Girl with the Golden Dress off the ground.

83 63 28
32 54 17
91 44 76

76 83 63

54 17 28

32 91 44

35:03

? ? ? ? ? ? ? ? ? ? ?

35:04

44 76 83

17 28 63

54 32 91

91 44 76

28 63 83

17 54 32

35:05

? ? ? ? ? ? ? ? ? ? ?

35:06

32 91 44

63 83 76

28 17 54

54 32 91
83 76 44
63 28 17

35:07

? ? ? ? ? ? ? ? ? ? ?

Light flare in center of screens.

35:08

17 54 32
76 44 91
83 63 28

28 17 54
44 91 32
76 83 63

35:09

? ? ? ? ? ? ? ? ? ? ?

35:10

63	28	17
91	32	54
44	76	83

83	63	28
32	54	17
91	44	76

Sound cue: *prepared piano, clanking, plucked strings.*

35:11

? ? ? ? ? ? ? ? ? ? ?

Girl with Black Hair and Girl in Sailor Hat carry their ectoplasmic photographs to Man in Striped Suit & Girl with the Golden Dress and display the photos to them. Girl with the Golden Dress turns away and toward the wall, then sits down and covers her eyes with her hands. Man in Striped Suit spins around to face the screens.

35:12

76	83	63
54	17	28
32	91	44

44 76 83
17 28 63
54 32 91

35:13

? ? ? ? ? ? ? ? ? ? ?

SCREENS – Japanese GIRL: "I understand you immediately when you say, knock, knock. I am hiding person. One, two, three, four. Help."

Deep Voice: Sta-sis.

Girl with Black Hair and Girl in Sailor Hat turn to face the screens.

35:21

I UNDERSTAND YOU IMMEDIATELY

Girl with Black Hair, Girl in Sailor Hat, and Girl with the Tiara walk toward Girl with the Golden Dress again, each carrying an ectoplasmic photograph.

35:31

I AM HIDING PERSON

Female Voice: *Votre imagination vous transporterez au pays de la vérité, et vous n'aurez plus à réflechir à tant de ces choses. Votre imagination vous transporterez au pays de la vérité, et vous n'aurez plus à réflechir à tant de ces choses.*

Girl with Black Hair, Girl in Sailor Hat, and Girl with the Tiara kneel on the ground and hold the photos in front of themselves. Girl with the Golden Dress rises and walks forward, stretching her hand out before her.

Voice: speech of distressed French woman continues, volume rising.

35:53 **SCREENS — WIPE TO CLOSE-UP OF:** girl crawling down stairs.

Girl with Black Hair, Girl in Sailor Hat, and Girl with the Tiara rise and walk offstage with the ectoplasmic photographs. Man in Striped Suit follows them, then stops at center stage.

36:07

"DEEP, DEEP, DOWN TO ....

... DIRTY NEW YORK CITY"

Man in Striped Suit places a stool in front of the stage-right small grand piano and stands on it and stares into the cylindrical object.

German Voice: *Ich will* (3x).

Voice: speech of distressed French woman fades out.

Music cue: *German industrial rock, Tarr music ends.*

36:28

THE VISITO
R IS ALWAY
S DEAD, AM
IDST THE E
XCTEMENT
OF THE EXP
ERIENCE TH
E VISITOR I
S ALWAYS D
EAD AMIDS
T THE EXCI
TEMENT OF

Male Voice: Here's the pro-po-sal: Never. [Whispered] May-be.

36:45 **SCREENS – WIPE TO CLOSE-UP OF:** girl sitting at bottom of stairwell.

Music cue: *gentle piano.*

36:56 **SCREENS – WIPE TO: JAPAN SCENE 6.** A Japanese woman in a pink dress walks up the stairs as the Japanese woman on the chair covers her eyes with her hands.

Male Voice: Sta-sis.

Man in Striped Suit walks behind the stage-right small grand piano, then sits behind it.

Sound cue: *hissing noise with overlapping distorted voices slowly increasing in volume.*

Male Voice: `Permanent. [Whispered] Da-mage.`

37:30 **SCREENS — X-FADE TO CLOSE-UP OF:** Japanese girl going up stairs.

Girl with the Tiara, Girl with the Golden Dress, Girl in Sailor Hat, and Girl with Black Hair enter with steak knives and pretend stabbing Man in Striped Suit.

37:33 **SCREENS — WIPE TO CLOSE-UP OF:** girl upstairs.

Male Voice (whispered): `May-be. May-be.`

Sound cue: *hissing noise continues, thunderous boom (9x).*

37:45 **SCREENS — X-FADE TO: JAPANESE GIRLS LOOKING OUT WINDOW.**

Girl with the Tiara, Girl in Sailor Hat, Girl in Golden Dress, and Girl with Black Hair walk to the stage-left wall and begin stabbing it with their knives.

Male Voice (whispered): `Be-cause ...`

38:02 **SCREENS — WIPE TO CLOSE-UP OF:** Japanese people walking downstairs.

Male Voice (whisper): `Nev-er.`

38:12 **SCREENS — CLOSE-UP OF JAPANESE GIRL.** She turns toward the camera.

Male Voice (commanding): `Look.`

38:20 **SCREENS – WIPE TO CLOSE-UP OF:** Japanese man looking.

Music cue: *gentle piano.*

38:27 **SCREENS – X-FADE TO ENGLAND: RED DRESS TABLEAU.** Two girls in red dresses, their arms around each other's backs. A man sits in front of them, his hands covering his mouth.

Male Voice: `Hands to paper heads... Hands to paper heads.`

Man in Striped Suit puts his hands to his mouth, then kneels at the edge of the stage-right small grand piano.

38:40 **SCREENS – X-FADE TO CLOSE-UP OF:** blonde English girl leaning back & closing her eyes.

Male Voice: `Emp-ty.`

38:48 **SCREENS – X-FADE TO:** three English women tearing apart paper hats then walking away and toward a door.

Male Voice: `Sing-ing my heart out. (Empty) That great ...`

39:00 **SCREENS – WIPE UP TO: ENGLAND SCENE 5.** A group of men in a red velvet room holding paintings of cows. A woman in the background stares at them.

Male Voice, continuing: `... jumping-off place. (Real) Here in – the beginning – of part two.`

GIRLS: Kachoo.

Music cue: *repeating single piano key, gentle piano.*

Male Voice: `Click.`

39:14 **SCREENS — WIPE TO: ENGLAND SCENE 5.** Two girls in black dresses embracing one another, then separating as men enter carrying paintings of cows.

Male Voice: `Second time. Singing my (empty) heart out.`

Music cue: *piano.*

39:24 **SCREENS — X-FADE TO BLACK.**

NOW
ON SOME
INFINITELY
DISTANT
PLANET

GIRLS: Kachoo (3x).

Male Voice: `But, but, but, why?`

39:33

WORK: THIS
IS WORK

Male Voice: `Look. Second time. Second time.`

Music cue: *German industrial rock.*

Male Voice: `Why now?`

39:41 **SCREENS – WIPE TO: JAPAN SCENE 7.** A corridor with windows. Playing cards are littered on the floor. A woman sits on a floral chair. A man sits further back from her facing the camera, one hand folded over his fist. In the background four men sit on a couch with their hands covering their faces while besides them men & women stand against the wall, also covering their faces.

Sound cue: *thunderous wood block clack (5x).*

Male Voice: `Absent.`

Music cue: *solo opera voice, solo clarinet.*

Girl with Black Hair, Girl in Tiara, Girl with the Golden Dress, and Girl in Sailor Hat lift up a large plastic Lacanian knot from the floor and place it against the stage-left wall.

39:53 **SCREENS – X-FADE TO CLOSE-UP OF:** Japanese man with cards.

Music cue: *solo clarinet.*

Male Voice: `No-thing in the heart, nothing in the mind –`

German Voice: *`Ich will.`*

Man in Striped Suit places a blindfold around Girl with the Tiara's eyes as Girl with the Golden Dress extends her arms in front of her and stares at the stage-right wall. Man in Striped Suit slaps his hand against his forehead.

Male Voice: `... in the be-hav-ior, no-thing in the head's business, (dou-ble wo-rld) no-thing in the ver-i-fi-a-ble` fact, `(ho-ver-ing) or the ver-i-fi-a-ble future.`

Music cue: *solo opera voice.*

Man in Striped Suit picks up the fabric from the floor and wraps it around his body.

MAN in Striped Suit: *Donde esta el baño, por favor.*

Sound cue: *nuclear alarm (3x); low humming.*

Male Voice: No re-la-tion-ship exists be-tween (click) what hap-pens on stage and what is hap-pen-ing on the il-lu-mi-na-ted screen except, suddenly – CLICK:

German Voice: *Ein klein-er Mensch.*

Male Voice, continuing: ... and a pro-found re-la-tion-ship does now ex-ist.

40:56 **SCREENS – WIPE TO CLOSE-UP OF:** Japanese boy & Japanese man in a blue robe holding playing cards. He drops the cards.

German Voice: *Ein klein-er Mensch.*

Male Voice: Click. It's that sim-ple.

Sound cue: *computer blip.*

Music cue: *opera, high-pitched buzz.*

41:07 **SCREENS – WIPE TO CLOSE-UP OF:** Japanese boy's face.

Girl in Tiara turns toward the audience, her hands covering her eyes. She remains still.

Male Voice: Ab-sent.

Music cue: *opera.*

Japanese WOMAN (off screen): "Doing everything twice."

Sound cue: *ding.*

41:23 **SCREENS – WIPE TO CLOSE-UP OF:** Japanese woman rubbing hands.

Music cue: *solo clarinet, thunderous boom.*

Male Voice: `I have been here be-fore you. (Hel-lo) I will be here after you have van-ished from my pri-vate men-tal world.`

Hummingbird enters & hovers in the stage-right corner.

41:40 **SCREENS – VERTICAL WIPE TO CLOSE-UP OF:** Japanese woman in front of boy. She turns toward the camera.

Sound cue: *nuclear alarm (3x).*

2

41:56 **SCREENS – WIPE TO CLOSE-UP OF:** Japanese woman in front of boy.

3

Japanese MAN: "You un-der-stand me im-me-di-ate-ly when I say, doing everything twice."

Woman (screaming): `1, 2, 3, 4! 1, 2, 3, 4!`

42:04 Girl with the Tiara spins around then covers her face with her hands.

Sound cue: *thunderous boom (9x).*

1 2 3
4 5 6
7 8 9

Male Voice: Do not dismiss, please, the possibility that, very soon, one eve-ning in this –

Music cue: *solo clarinet.*

42:24 **SCREENS – WIPE TO JAPAN SCENE 7.**

Girl with the Tiara lowers her hands, thereby removing the blindfold from her eyes, then turns back toward the screen and quickly walks to it & places her hands on it.

Male Voice, continuing: ... series of eve-nings, it may hap-pen, that a single in-di-vi-dual, (damage) present at this very performance may, he or she, lock into the eve-ning's form-al fluc-tu-a-tions.

SCREENS – Japanese WOMAN: "I understand you immediately when you say, doing everything twice be-cause, this is always true."

German Voice (repeating continuously): *Eins, zwei, drei, vier.*

Girl with the Tiara retreats from the screen, turns toward audience, then turns back toward the screen and places her hands on it.

Sound cue: *ringing phone.*

43:00 **SCREENS — WIPE DOWN TO CLOSE-UP OF LIGHT-BULB.**

1 2 3
4 5 6
7 8 9

Woman (screaming): One, two, three, four!

Girl with the Tiara raises her hands in the air then runs to the screen as if trying to run through it but smashes against the wall. She bounces back and retreats to behind the scroll stand. Her shadow extends across the left screen.

Screens fade to blank.

Sound cue: *ringing phone.*

Male Voice: Spea-king dead always through spea-king.

43:19 **SCREENS — X-FADE TO: JAPAN SCENE 7.** An old wood-paneled courtroom.

ONE

Japanese MAN: "You un-der-stand me im-me-di-ate-ly, when I say:"

Girl with the Tiara turns back and forth, staring at the left screen, then at the audience.

Male Voice: Sta-sis.

Japanese WOMAN: "I understand you im-me-di-ate-ly when you say, doing everything twice, because this is always true."

Bulb flash.

43:29

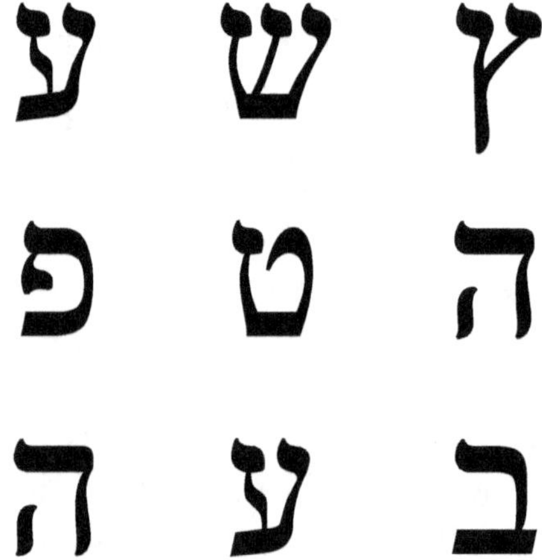

Girl with the Tiara repeatedly slams herself against the upstage screen as if trying to penetrate it.

Music cue: *screeching violin.*

Woman (screaming): `One, two, three, four! 1, 2, 3, 4!`

Japanese MAN: "Doing everything twice, tick tock, tick tock."

Sound cue: *computerized machine-gun blast, nuclear alarm (3x).*

43:38 Girl with the Tiara runs upstage and swiftly thrusts her upper body into the cylindrical object.

2

3

43:50

YOUR OWN
PICTURE
HERE ON
THIS SCREEN
$25 ONLY

Music cue: *funereal organ.*

Girl in Sailor Hat walks to the cabinet, retrieves an object from the cabinet, then stares at the screens. She returns to the stage-left wall and stretches her arms upwards along it.

Male Voice: `Yes, no.`

44:05 **SCREENS – VERTICAL WIPE TO: JAPAN SCENE. A group of men in black suits sitting under a window; next to them, on each side, stand several women in dresses.**

Man in Striped Suit stares at the audience, then walks to the stage-left wall and extends his arms upwards, placing his hands over those of Girl in Sailor Hat.

Male Voice: `Real. Dou-ble world. Never.`

SCREENS – JAPAN SCENE: The Japanese people standing against the wall cover their faces with their hands.

Male Voice: Look.

Girl in Sailor Hat walks away from the wall toward Girl with the Tiara, then escorts her away.

44:56 **SCREENS – ZOOM OUT: JAPAN SCENE.** Long wide hallway. A Japanese woman is sitting in a chair and facing the camera. A Japanese man several feet behind her is also sitting in a chair staring at the camera. In the background are four Japanese men in suits covering their faces with their hands; beside them, against each wall, stand other Japanese people covering their faces with their hands.

Male Voice: Hel-lo. Click.

Man in Striped Suit removes a white object from the cabinet.

Male Voice: No such thing. (Empty) No such thing. No such thing.

Sound cue: *computer blip (3x).*

Man in Striped Suit unravels the white fabric to reveal a fish, which he displays to the audience. The fabric contains vertical lines of Hebrew letters. He holds the fish under his chin.

MAN in Striped Suit (in gruff voice): *Ba-ruch a-tah A-do-nai eloheinu mel-ech ha'olam.*

Male Voice: Click. Re-al.

Music cue: *modernist opera.*

45:47 **SCREENS – JAPAN SCENE.** All Japanese people rise to exit but remain at the very edge of the screen.

Male Voice: Speak-ing dead, always. Hiding now from every dou-ble world.

Music cue: *solo opera voice, gentle piano.*

Sound cue: *nuclear alarm (2x).*

46:06 **SCREENS – FADE TO BLACK.**

ONLY BEING
A TOURIST
CAN ONE
EXPERIENCE
A PLACE

Woman (screaming): One, two, three, four!

46:09 **SCREENS – X-FADE TO CLOSE-UP OF:** blonde English girl sleeping.

Male Voice: Ab-sent.

GIRL in Sailor Hat (singing): I wish ... I was ... a sail-or ..... who cha-ses all the girls.

Sound cue: *computer blip (3x).*

46:31 **SCREENS – WIPE TO: ENGLAND SCENE 6.** Ensemble of men & women sleeping on a couch.

Male Voice: Emp-ty. The feel-ing of no feel-ing.

GIRL in Sailor Hat (singing): I prom-ise – I will – hurt – them.

46:50 **SCREENS — WIPE TO: ENGLAND SCENE 6.**

Male Voice: `No such thing.`

Sound cue: *ringing phone.*

Male Voice: `Pause.`

> **SCREENS** — English **MAN**: "The forgotten premise: tick, tock. Tick, tock."
>
> Girl with the Tiara moves slowly across the stage with the fabric.

47:04 **SCREENS — WIPE TO: ENGLAND SCENE 6.** A woman in a black dress walks back and forth across the foreground.

Male Voice: `O-pen this door.`

47:06 **SCREENS — WIPE TO: ENGLAND SCENE 6.** A shadow crosses the screen again and again.

Male Voice: `Click. May-be.`

47:15 **SCREENS — WIPE TO: ENGLAND SCENE 6.** The English people rise and exit. Shadows continue to pass across the screens.

Male Voice (whispered): `Pose. Pose for me.`

> GIRL with the Tiara (singing, very slowly): "Me."

Male Voice: `Ab-sent. Beginning.`

> GIRL with the Tiara (continuing to sing): "... and my sha-."
> Man in Striped Suit stomps on the ground, startling Girl with the Tiara, interrupting her singing.

47:52 **SCREENS — FROM BLACK FADE IN TO: ENGLAND SCENE 6.**

20

Male Voice: The following mental experiment may help.

47:57 **SCREENS — FADE TO BLACK.**

Male Voice: First time.

25

Male Voice: Al-ways. (Double) Imagine a pill named O-X.

48:00 **SCREENS — FADE IN TO: ENGLAND SCENE 6. SLEEPING.**

Male Voice: Taken every day, for a period of a year.

48:03 **SCREENS — FADE TO BLACK.**

27

Male Voice: And just once each day, in the 24 hours of its effectiveness, it links the perceived data of a specific, ordinary moment to universal truth. (Prom-i-ses.)

48:07 **SCREENS – WIPE TO CLOSE-UP OF: ENGLISH GIRLS SLEEPING.**

Man in Striped Suit takes a pill from the bowl on the small grand piano, slowly turns, stands center stage, swallows the pill, then covers his mouth with his hands. Girl in Sailor Hat walks to the cabinet.

Lights go dark.

Male Voice: `Start here again. Pause.`

48:27 **SCREENS – WIPE TO CLOSE-UP OF: BRUNETTE ENGLISH GIRL.** English GIRL: "Knock, knock, knock. I wasn't looking, when it happened."

Male Voice: `Sta-sis. Look-ing.`

48:40 **SCREENS – WIPE TO CLOSE-UP OF:** dark-haired English girl. She raises her head slowly & stares into the distance.

Male Voice: `Hi-ding now from ev-ery (may-be) double world.`

Girl with the Golden Dress and Girl in Sailor Hat lift the fabric and wrap Girl with the Tiara in it, then unwrap her.

Music cue: *piano.*

Male Voice: `Beginning.`

49:01 **SCREENS – X-FADE TO:** blonde British woman wearing paper hat.

Male Voice: `Dam-age. The arena in which –`

Girl in Sailor Hat performs song variations vamping on the word "Damage."

49:10 **SCREENS — WIPE TO CLOSE-UP OF:** upside-down Japanese woman.

Girl with the Golden Dress walks to the cabinet. She removes one of the drawers then places it on Girl with the Tiara's head.

Male Voice: `Go to England. First time. And, ahhh, the great giants of mys-ti-cism did not say this ex-act thing. Go to Japan. Second time. Sta-sis.`

Music cue (low, then rising in volume): *funky organ jazz.*

49:26 **SCREENS — WIPE TO CLOSE-UP OF:** Japanese man. Japanese MAN: "My choice. Tick, tock."

Male Voice: `Sta-sis.`

49:32 **SCREENS — WIPE TO CLOSE-UP OF:** Japanese boy & Japanese man with ripped-open paper hat.

Male Voice: `And the an-cient deep think-ers did not say this ex-act thing.`

MAN in Striped Suit: *¿Dónde esta el baño? ¡El baño!*

Music cue: *funky organ jazz continues.*

Girl with Black Hair thrusts her steak knife back and forth in the air above the stage-left small grand piano. Girl with the Golden Dress thrusts her knife over the head of Girl with the Tiara, who begins screaming, then runs away & faints with the drawer in hand. Girl with the Golden Dress runs after her and also faints.

GIRL with Black Hair (singing): Ahhhhhhhhhhh, bad, bad, bad boy.

GIRL with the Tiara: I am seriously hurt!

GIRL with the Golden Dress: Japan! Japan!

Deep Voice: Looking at me, reading my thoughts, imitating my voice, my gestures, my best ideas.

49:41 **SCREENS — WIPE TO: JAPAN SCENE 9.** A Japanese man & two Japanese women in a white room. Each of their heads are wrapped in newspaper.

GIRL in Sailor Hat vamping: Sail-or boys from En-gland have Jap-a-nese ro-mance.

Male Voice: Sta-sis.

GIRL in Sailor Hat: *Kon-i-chi-wa*! Bee-bee-beep!

Male Voice: Hov-er-ing.

Sound cue: *siren.*

Male Voice: Hovering ... Ahhh. The great giants of mysticism (da-mage) did not say this ex-act thing ... And the ancient deep thinkers did not say this ex-act thing ... [sound cue: *computer blip (2x)*] which, is true on some infinitely distant planet.

Girl with Black Hair takes a white pill from the glass bowl on the small grand piano and holds it in the air while staring at the audience, then finally places it on her tongue and slowly draws it into her mouth.

Male Voice: First time. Second time.

50:47 **SCREENS — WIPE TO: JAPAN SCENE 9.**

Male Voice: Never. O-kay. Looking at me, imitating my thoughts, imitating my voice, my gestures, my best ideas.

Sound cue: *loud knock (2x).*

Male Voice: Here's the pro-po-sal. O-K.

50:57 **SCREENS — X-FADE TO:** English girls in red dresses.

Sound cue: *loud knock.*

Music cue: *eerie organ.*

Male Voice: `Imagine a pill –`

51:05 **SCREENS — WIPE UP TO: JAPAN SCENE 9.** A group of three men in black suits sitting before a woman in a red dress and beret in a dark room. One of the men is blindfolded, another holds up an object. The woman holds her hands over her belly and looks downward.

Male Voice, continuing: `... named O-X –`

French voice: *`Extraordinaire.`*

51:18 **SCREENS — WIPE TO: JAPAN SCENE 9.** Panels in the background open. Four women and a man enter and point toward the camera, then hold up their palms.

Girl with Black Hair crosses her hands in front of her face, then slowly turns her head and walks to the cylindrical object.

Male Voice, continuing: `... taken every day for a period of a year, and just once each day in the 24 hours of its effectiveness –`

Sound cue: *war siren, machine-gun blast.*

Girl with the Golden Dress and Girl with Black Hair lift the cylindrical object & begin placing it in a cubicle in the stage-right wall, then hold it at a tilted angle while they stare at the screens.

Sound cue: *siren.*

51:32

DEAD PEOP
LE ARE NE
VER DEAD
IF LIVING
PEOPLE A
RE DEAD W
HEN THEY
ARE LIVIN
G AND NO
T DEAD W
HEN THEY
ARE DEAD

Male Voice: May-be now ...

SCREENS – Japanese MAN: "You understand me im-me-di-ate-ly when I say, everything is a reminding. Knock, knock, knock."

Male Voice: Go to o-ther worlds.

Girl with the Golden Dress & Girl with Black Hair place the object in the cubicle.

Female Voice (sung): Ear-ly in the mor-ning ... Ear-ly in the mor-ning.

Male Voice: Yes, no. Yes, no.

Female Voice: *Votre imagination vous transporterez au pays de la vérité, et vous n'aurez plus à réflechir à tant de ces choses.*

Male Voice: But, but, why? Why now?

Music cue: *solo opera voice.*

Sound cue: *low humming.*

52:00 **SCREENS – WIPE TO: JAPAN SCENE 9.** The panels have been completely opened to reveal a large spacious room. Against the wall in the background stand a woman in a white dress & a green jacket and a woman dressed in black.

Male Voice: Click.

Girl with the Golden Dress walks across the stage and kneels before Girl with the Tiara and Girl in Sailor Hat, who are both staring at the audience, each holding their left legs out and placing their hands on their hips.

Male Voice: And just once each day in the 24 hours of its effectiveness, it links the perceived da-ta of a specific ordinary moment to universal truth.

Music cue: *mysterious piano, solo opera voice.*

52:23 **SCREENS – X-FADE TO CLOSE-UP OF:** Japanese girls leaning against the wall.

Male Voice: Look. And, ahhh, the great giants of mys-ticism did not say this exact thing.

Male Voice: And as you can per-haps imagine –

Sound cue: *computer blip.*

52:29 **SCREENS – WIPE TO JAPAN SCENE 9:** wide shot of leaning girls.

Male Voice, continuing: ... this means that the pill-taker lives in a con-stant state of watch-ful ten-sion,

Male Voice: And the ancient deep thinkers did not say this exact thing.

Sound cue: *computer blip.*

Girl with Black Hair takes another pill.

52:44 **SCREENS — WIPE TO JAPAN SCENE 9.** The girls in the background and the group all faint. A man leans against a pole, hugging it.

Male Voice, continuing: ... hope-ful of being able to recognize that otherwise unexceptional moment which is, in fact, exceptional.

Music cue: *mysterious piano continues.*

Girl in Sailor Hat and Girl with the Tiara walk to Man in Striped Suit and lift him off the ground.

Male Voice: Start here a-gain.

Girl in Sailor Hat lifts Man in Striped Suit's tie and pretends cutting it in half with her hand.

Male Voice: Emp-ty.

53:03 Man in Striped Suit walks away, wraps his hand around a pole, stares at the upstage screen.

\+ + + +

\+ + + +

\+ + + +

53:10

X X X X

X X X X

X X X X

Music cue: *piano.*

> **SCREENS** – Japanese **BOY** (sung): "I hear you knock-ing, but you can't get in."

Sound cue: *war siren, thunderous boom (4x).*

53:19

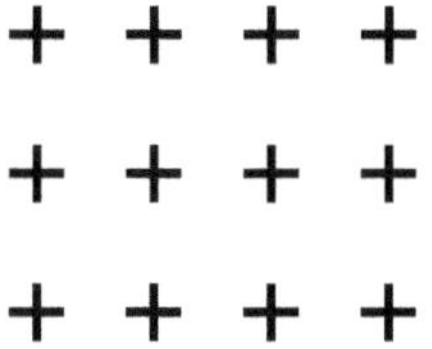

53:27

? ? ? ? ? ? ? ? ? ? ?

Male Voice (whispered): `May-be. Click.`

> Man in Striped Suit walks away from the pole toward the small grand piano, which he drags slightly to stage left, then sits behind.

Male Voice: `Go to other levels immediately. Please, please.`

Music cue: *German industrial rock.*

Girl in Sailor Hat and Girl with the Tiara creep toward Man in Striped Suit while gingerly dangling playing cards in their hands.

MAN in Striped Suit: Please, please.

Sound cue: *nuclear alarm (3x).*

Male Voice: `The mean-ing, the mean-ing, the mean-ing is in the mem-o-ry bank.`

Sound cue: *boom.*

Each of the Girls holds a playing card up to her face and slowly turns it back & forth, then covers her left eye with the card at a diagonal angle. They remain still, holding this position.

Male Voice: `Double.`

54:25 **SCREENS – VERTICAL WIPE TO: JAPAN SCENE 10.** A Japanese woman sits in a plush chair with an elegant pillow beneath her head. A Japanese man in a hat is sitting behind her, partly concealed by a sliding screen door.

ALL of the actors (whispering): No.

YOU UNDERSTAND ME IMMEDIATELY WHEN I SAY..........................

FIRST BUT ONLY FIRST................

SCREENS – Japanese GIRL: "You understand me immediately when I say, first, but only first, only tick tock."

Male Voice: `May-be now ..... Full say-ing lies .....`

All actresses lower their cards then bend & sway their hips backwards in unison.

54:49 **SCREENS – VERTICAL WIPE TO: JAPAN SCENE 10.** Shift to partial view of room with man in hat sitting by the sliding panel door. Behind him are three men kneeling on the tatami floor. They throw stuffed animals into the air then rise, slowly walk, then collapse.

Male Voice: `May-be now. May-be.`

Sound cue: *loud thunderous boom.*

All of the actresses jerk their hips to the left in unison to the accompanying sound cue of a *loud thunderous boom*, then turn toward the screens then back toward the audience, gesturing with their cards & screaming.

Music cue: *strident violin.*

Music cue: *German industrial rock.*

All of the actresses surround Man in Striped Suit and kneel before him with their cards, then spin in circles.

MAN in Striped Suit: *¿Dónde esta el baño? El baño por favor.*

55:13 All of the actresses scream, bark, and strut across the stage with their playing cards, holding them above their heads as they stare at the upstage screens. They bark repeatedly in high-pitched tones.

REAL JAPAN

Female Voice (screaming): 1, 2, 3, 4.

Music cue: *German industrial rock.*

55:24 **SCREENS – WIPE TO CLOSE-UP OF:** Japanese men with dolls. They throw them into the air then slowly walk forward and collapse.

Male Voice: Damage.

Music cue: *piano loop.*

Male Voice: Nothing in the heart; in the behavior; nothing in the head's business; nothing in the ver-i-fi-a-ble fact, or the ver-i-fi-a-ble fu-ture.

Sound cue: *nuclear alarm (3x).*

Girl in Tiara & Girl in Sailor Hat turn away from the wall and make cheerleader-like moves, bending down, standing up, and spinning around with the playing cards in their hands.

Female Voice (screaming): 1, 2, 3, 4.

ALL stage actors (shouting): Don't You.

German Voice: *Ich will. Ich will.*

French voice: *A-mer-i-ca, A-mer-i-ca, A-mer-i-ca, A-mer-i-ca.*

Girl in Tiara and Girl in Sailor Hat slowly turn back toward the stage-left wall and lean against it.

German Voice (singing): *Ich ha-be dich. Ich ha-be dich.*

55:50 **SCREENS — WIPE TO CLOSE-UP OF:** Japanese girl with hat.

Male Voice: Start here a-gain.

Man in Striped Suit drags the stage-left small grand piano slightly to the side by the lid, then pulls a red fabric from within the piano & covers the instrument.

55:54 **SCREENS — WIPE DOWN TO CLOSE-UP OF:** Japanese girl with knife. She holds it against her cheek, pointing the knife just beneath her eye.

Male Voice: Never.

SCREENS — Japanese GIRL: "Tick, tock; tick, tock."

Man in Striped Suit bends down to kiss the small grand piano then spins around to stare at the screens.

Male Voice: The arena, the arena in which no promises are made.

Music cue: *gentle piano, low buzzing.*

Male Voice: Go to New York City. Immediately, immediately.

56:09 **SCREENS — X-FADE TO:** English girls in red dresses and the man covering his mouth with his hands.

Girl with the Tiara takes two fish out of the cabinet and hands them to Girl in Sailor Hat, who holds them gingerly by the tail and displays them to the audience.

56:26 **SCREENS – FADE TO BLACK.**

Girl with the Tiara takes another object from the cabinet and gingerly walks with it to center stage. She unveils the object, which is a fish. Girl with Black Hair stands next to her and stares at the fish. Girl in Sailor Hat holds the fish aloft.

Male Voice: Stasis.

56:36 **SCREENS – WIPE TO CLOSE-UP OF:** woman bandaging a man's arm.

YOUNG ENGLISH PEOPLE WHO UNDERSTAND ....

? ? ? ? ? ? ? ? ? ? ?

Male Voice: Permanent. Da-mage.

Girl with the Golden Dress approaches the group of girls, takes the fish from Girl with the Tiara, then spins around to display it to the audience.

THE ENEM
Y OF WOR
DS HIDDE
N INSIDE
WORDS T
HE ENEM
Y OF WOR
DS HIDDE
N INSIDE
WORDS T
HE ENEM
Y OF WOR

56:53 **SCREENS – WIPE TO CLOSE-UP OF:** Japanese woman. She turns so that only the back of her head is visible.

Girl with the Golden Dress walks in a circle with the fish till she reaches the screens. Girl in Sailor Hat and Girl with Black Hair follow her as Man in Striped Suit bends next to the small grand piano and kisses it.

56:55 **SCREENS – WIPE TO CLOSE-UP OF:** hands behind back.

Sound cue: *throbbing noise.*

Music cue: *solo opera voice.*

Girl with the Golden Dress stands motionless before the upstage screens, staring at the images.

57:05 **SCREENS — JAPAN SCENE 11. WIPE TO CLOSE-UP OF:** the back of the Japanese woman, who is holding a piece of fabric in her hands.

Sound cue: *ringing phone.*

Girl with the Tiara slowly creeps across the stage and places a small sledgehammer on the floor before Man in Striped Suit.

Male Voice: Damage. O-pen this door. O-pen this door. Look. Nev-er.

Music cue: *solo clarinet, carousel tune.*

French Voice: *Ex-traor-di-naire.*

57:36 **SCREENS — WIPE TO: JAPAN SCENE 11.** The woman walks forward with the fabric. A group of men and women stand against the wall holding their hands in prayer. A woman in a black dress continues to bandage a man's arm. Another woman kneels before them but stares toward the camera.

French Voice: *Ex-traor-di-naire. Ex-traor-di-naire.*

Girl with Black Hair lifts the red fabric that Man in Striped Suit has put on the small grand piano. She holds the fabric, takes another white pill from the glass jar hidden under it.

Music cue: *prepared piano, plucked strings, clanking.*

57:53

YOU UNDERSTAND ME IMMEDIATE-LY WHEN I SAY.........................

Male Voice: `Al-ways.`

> **SCREENS** – Japanese **WOMAN** (turning toward the camera): "You understand me im-me-di-ate-ly when I say, having forgotten this thing, knock, knock, it's me."

Sound cue: *war siren, woodblock clack, machine-gun blast.*

Woman (screaming): `One, two, three, four!`

58:12 Man in Striped Suit turns from the audience toward the screens, slams the sledgehammer against his head, faints.

DO NOT FOR
GET THOSE
WHO TRAVE
L TO A PLAC
E FROM WHI
CH THERE IS
NO RETURN
BECAUSE T
HE END OF
ALL EXPERI
ENCES DO N
OT FORGET

Male Voice: `Al-ways.`

Sound cue: *machine-gun blast repeating continuously.*

Girl with Black Hair covers the small grand piano, walks to center stage, picks up the sledgehammer, stares at the audience, then spins around to face the screens, then spins back to face the audience. She flips the sledgehammer from hand to hand.

Music cue: *1920s carousel jazz.*

Girl with Black Hair walks to Man in Striped Suit, taps him on the shoulder, then pretends slamming the sledgehammer against her head. Man in Striped Suit faints.

Woman (screaming): One, two, three, four!

Girl with Black Hair moves back and forth in different directions, stares at the screens, spins back around and while facing the audience, pretends slamming the sledgehammer against her head again.

Male Voice: Big girls ... big girls don't cry.

Girl with the Tiara hands Girl with Black Hair a bouquet of flowers. Girl with Black Hair walks away, tosses the flowers on the ground, then turns back to the screens and stares at them. Girl with the Tiara raises her hands to her face as if to cry. Girl with the Golden Dress picks up the scepter and rattles it at the screens.

Woman (screaming): One, two, three, four!

Sound cue: *ringing phone.*

58:48

BIG GIRLS
DON'T CRY

58:50 **SCREENS — WIPE TO CLOSE-UP OF:** Japanese woman.

Male Voice: `First time. Second time.`

59:01

OPEN THIS DOOR

Girl with Black Hair slowly raises her right arm and points at the screens.

French Voice: *Ex-traor-di-naire. Ex-traor-di-naire.*

59:07 **SCREENS — X-FADE TO CLOSE-UP OF:** woman outside.

[flashing on & off]

OPEN THIS DOOR

59:16 **SCREENS — WIPE TO: JAPAN #11B.** The woman turns toward the camera.

Male Voice: `Third time.`

[flashing on & off]

OPEN THIS DOOR

Girl with Black Hair turns and stares at the audience & puts her finger to her lips to shush them.

59:30 **SCREENS** – all of the praying people fall to their knees. The woman continues to bandage the man.

YOU UNDERSTAND ME IMMEDIATELY WHEN I SAY........................

Sound cue: *computer blip (7x).*

Male Voice: `And just once each day.`

Girl in Sailor Hat walks to the stage-right small grand piano and places her hands on the keys then stares back at the audience. Girl with the Tiara repeats the same actions.

59:36 **SCREENS – WIPE TO CLOSE-UP OF:** Japanese woman slowly walking toward the camera. She turns away.

YOU UNDERSTAND ME IMMEDIATELY WHEN I SAY........................

Male Voice: `And just once each day. Hi-ding now.`

Girl in Sailor Hat removes her hands from the small grand piano then places them over her breasts *&* stares at the audience. She remains still.

59:52 **SCREENS — X-FADE TO CLOSE-UP OF:** Japanese woman outside. She turns back toward the camera.

1:00:01 **SCREENS — WIPE TO CLOSE-UP OF:** Japanese woman. Slowly, she walks toward the camera.

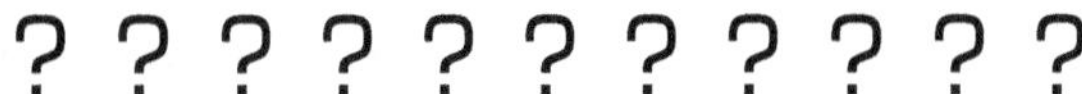

[timer counting from 1 to 14 above final "?"]

? ? ? ? ? ? ? ? ? ? ? ?

Girl with Black Hair slowly turns about and kneels before the right side of the stage-right small grand piano then turns toward the audience. Girl in Golden Dress does the exact same movements. They remain still.

1:00:03 **SCREENS — WIPE TO CLOSE-UP OF: JAPANESE WOMAN.**

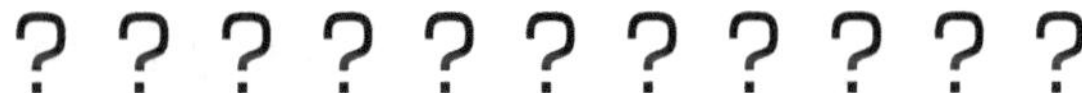

[timer counting from 14 to 22 above final "?"]

? ? ? ? ? ? ? ? ? ? ? ?

Sound cue: *low hum rising in pitch.*

1:00:21 **SCREENS — WIPE TO CLOSE-UP OF:** crying Japanese woman.

? ? ? ? ? ? ? ? ? ? ?

[timer counting from 23 to 37 above final "?"]

? ? ? ? ? ? ? ? ? ? ? ?

Sound cue: *humming noise.*

Music cue: *piano.*

1:00:49 **SCREENS – X-FADE TO**: closed theater curtain.

Music cue: *gentle piano.*

Girl in Sailor Hat and Girl with the Tiara both take a white pill.

1:01:05 **SCREENS – X-FADE TO CLOSE-UP OF**: dark-haired girl. A series of bodies swiftly walk back and forth across the screen creating shadows across the girl's face.

Music cue: *solo opera voice.*

Male Voice: `A mi-nute and im-per-cep-ti-ble short-circuit in hu-man life.`

Sound cue: *computer blip (repeating).*

Girl in Sailor Hat and Girl with the Tiara faint.

Male Voice: `Al-ways. Al-ways.`

Sound cue: *computer blip (3x).*

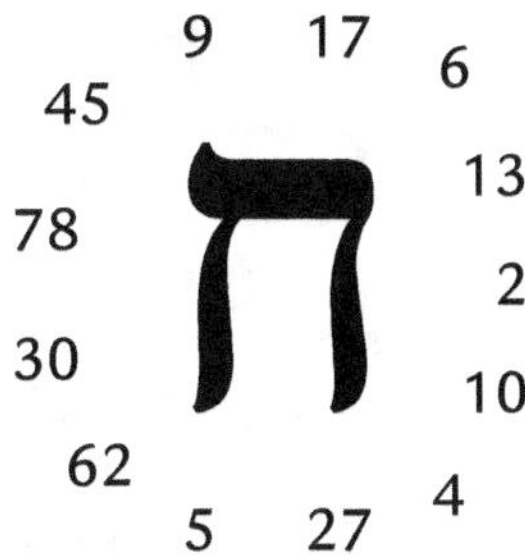

[sequence shifts six times (the numbers moving clockwise) to *computer blip* sound cue]

1:01:35 **SCREENS – X-FADE TO:** open theater curtain.

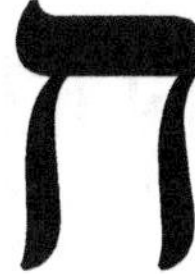

1:01:41 **SCREENS – X-FADE TO CLOSE-UP OF:** Japanese man and woman in chair, each of whom eventually collapses, falling to the ground in slow motion.

Girl with the Golden Dress and Girl with Black Hair quickly rise, walk upstage, then suddenly faint.

1:01:57 **SCREENS – WIPE TO BLACK.**

Music cue: *1920s carousel jazz (plays out till end).*

1:02:11

LADIES
AND
GENTLEMEN

1:02:24

THE
ACTORS
ARE
ONLY
RESTING

1:02:36

HOWEVER
THE
PERFORMANCE
IS
NOW
OVER

1:02:50

PLEASE
FEEL
FREE
TO
LEAVE
THE
THEATER

1:03:03

REMEMBER
THE
ACTORS
ARE
SIMPLY
RESTING

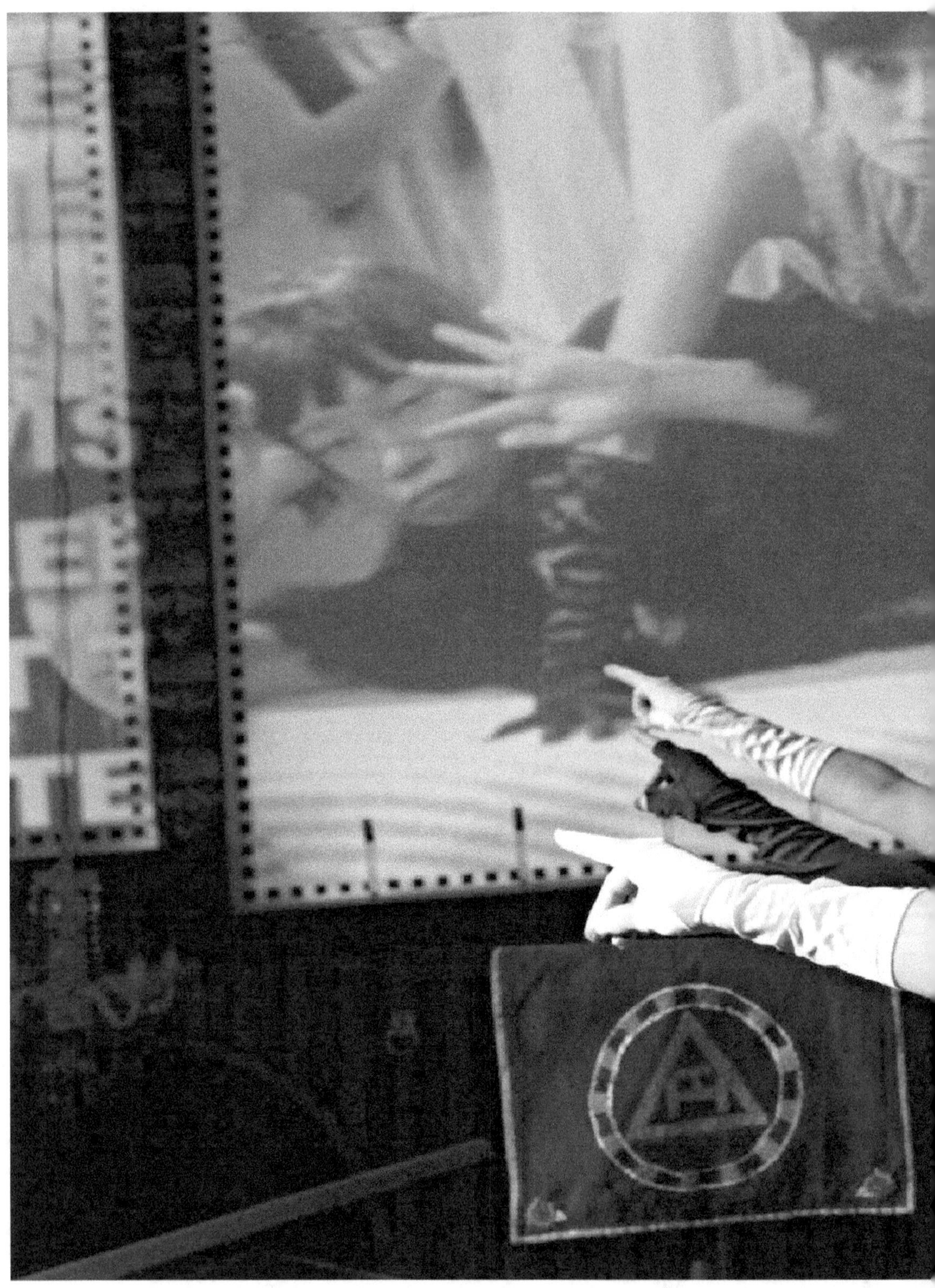

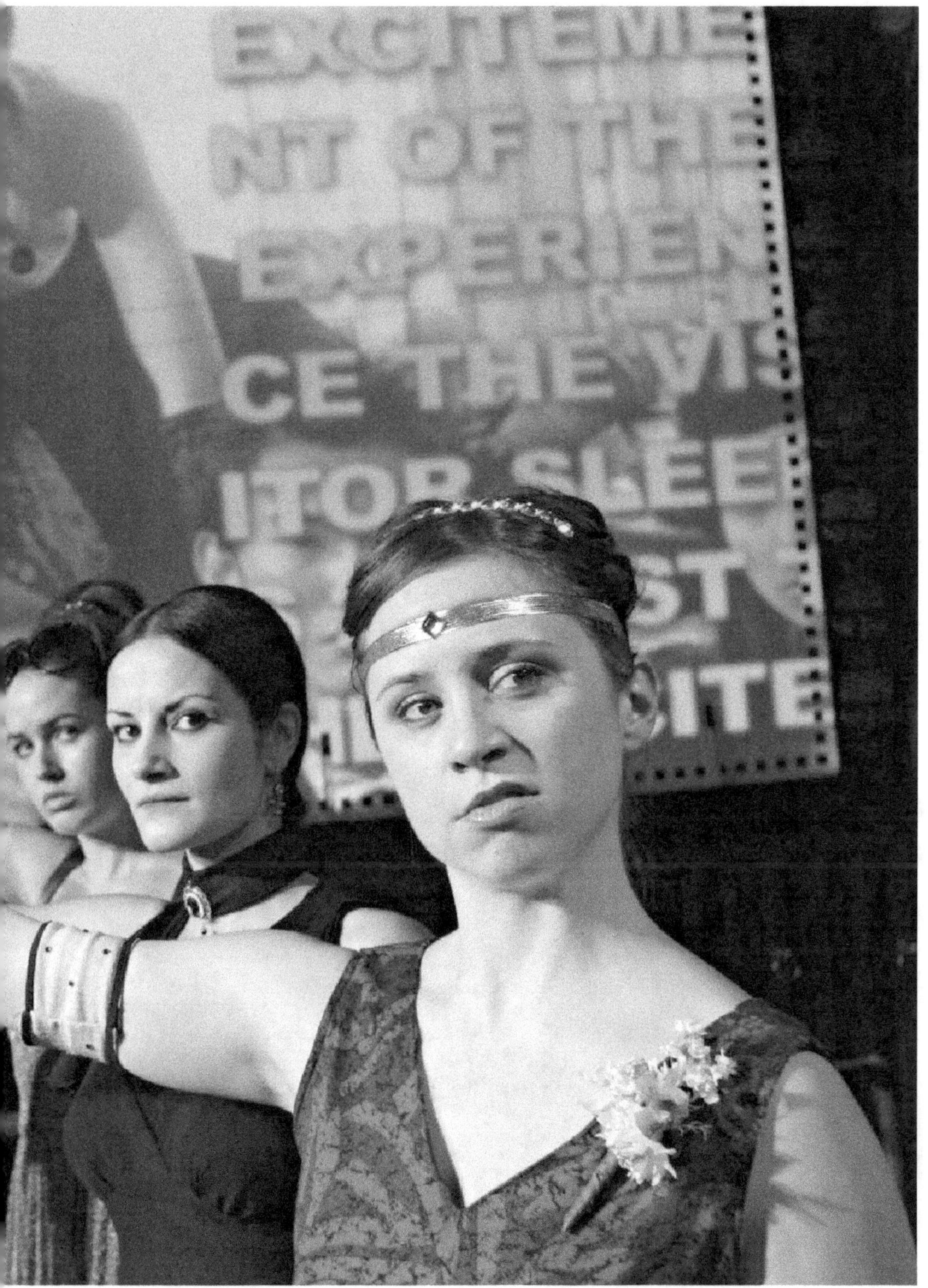
EXCITEME
NT OF THE
EXPERIEN
CE THE VIS
ITOR SLEE
ST
ITE

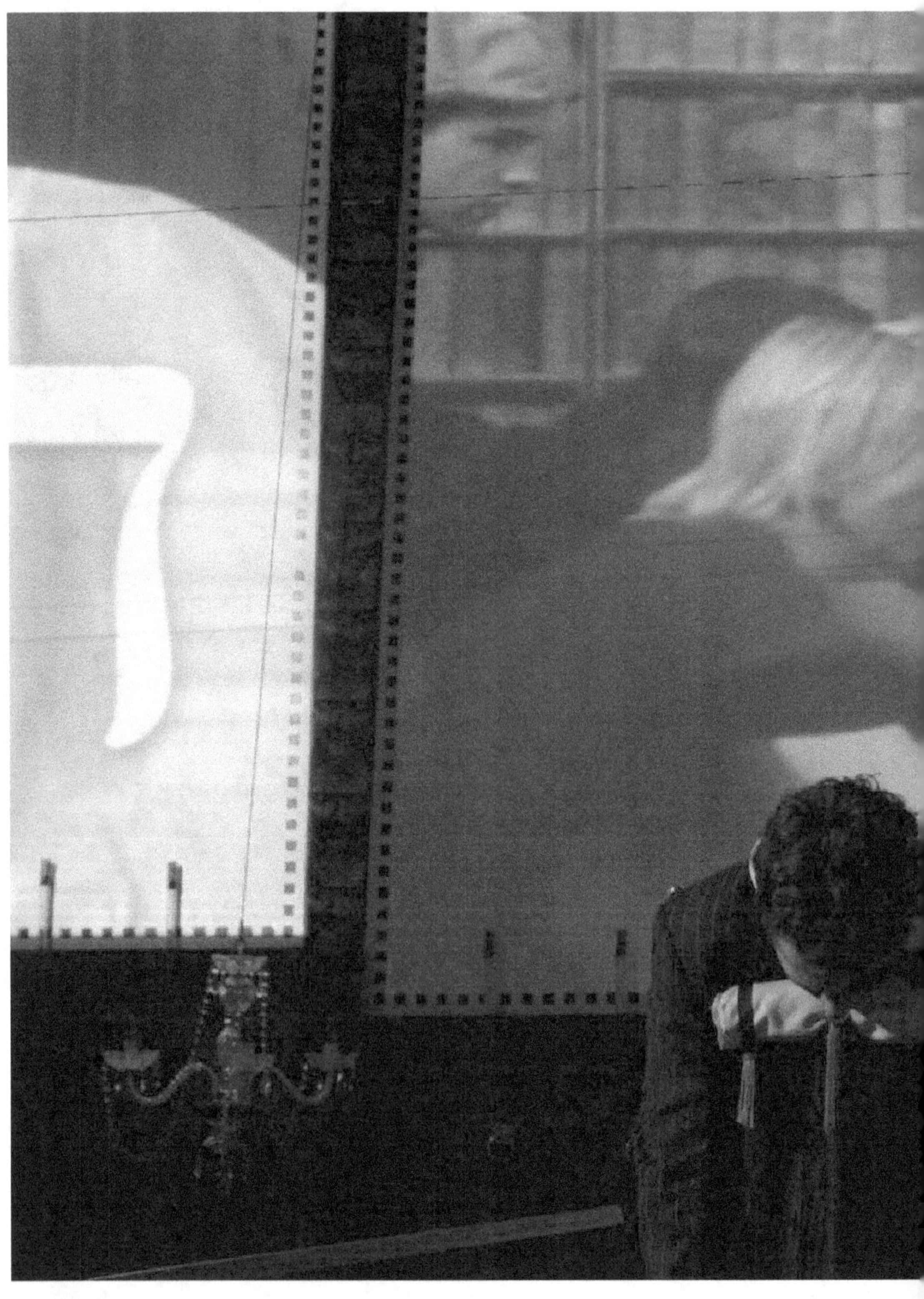

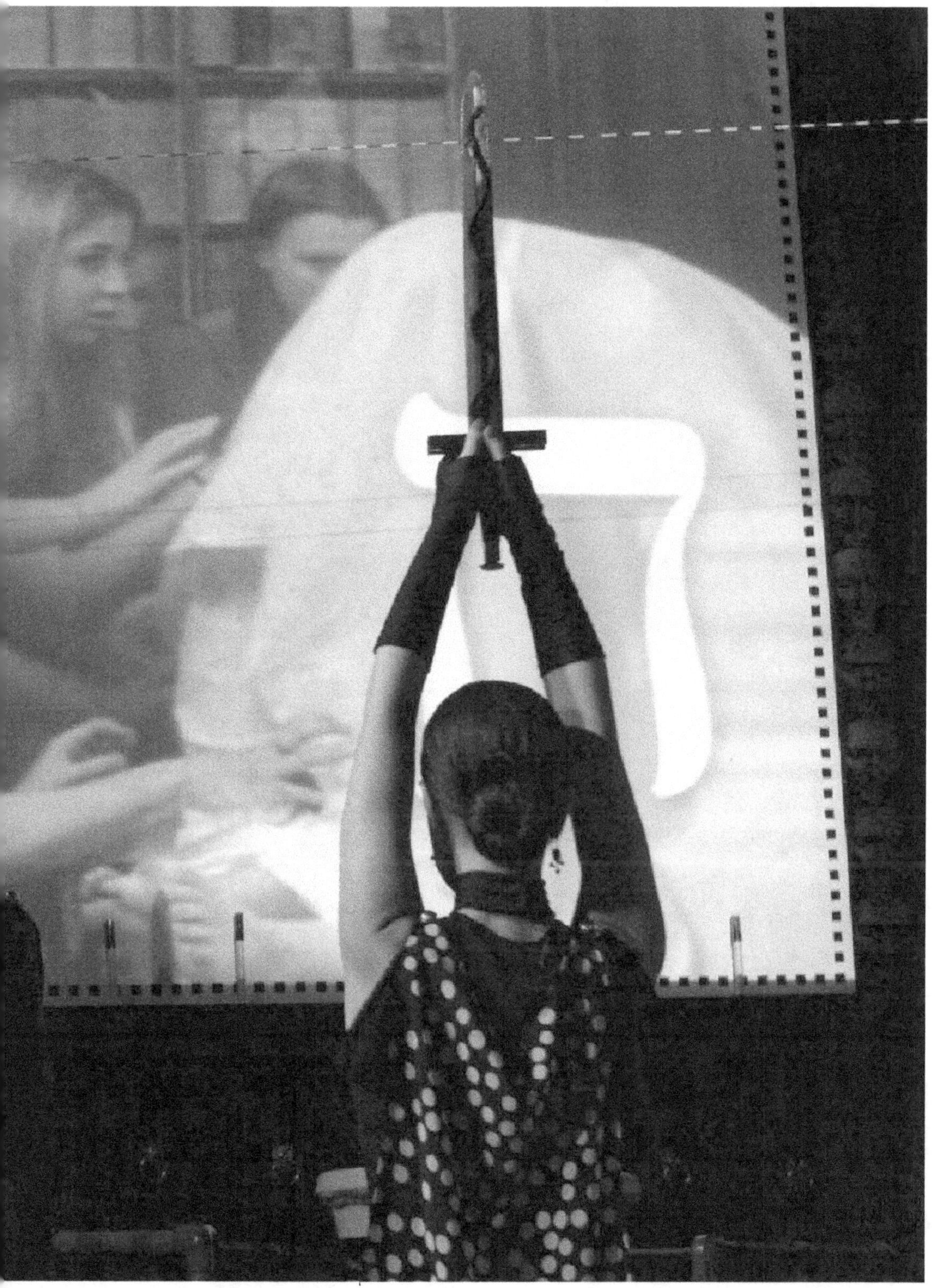

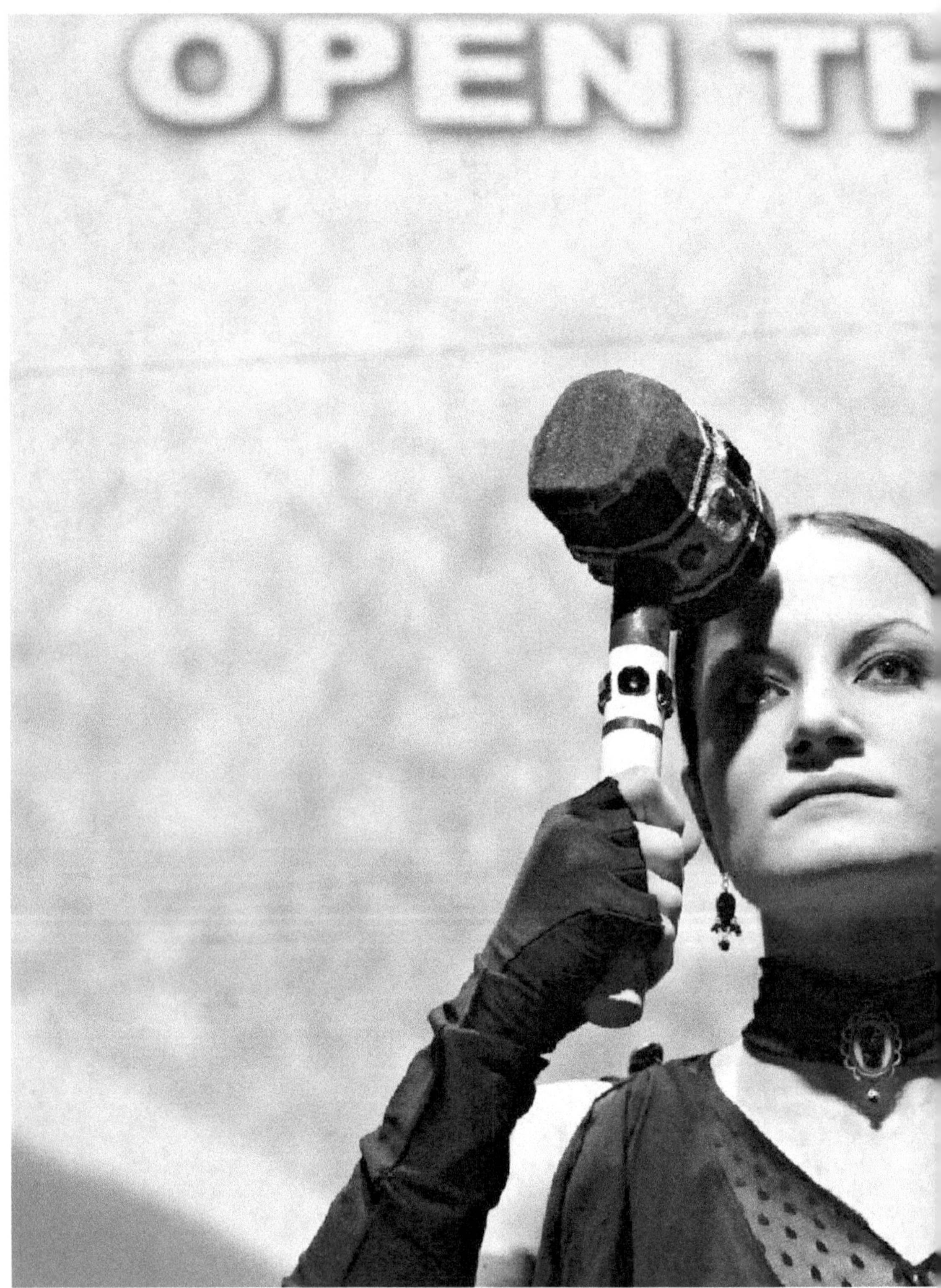
OPEN TH

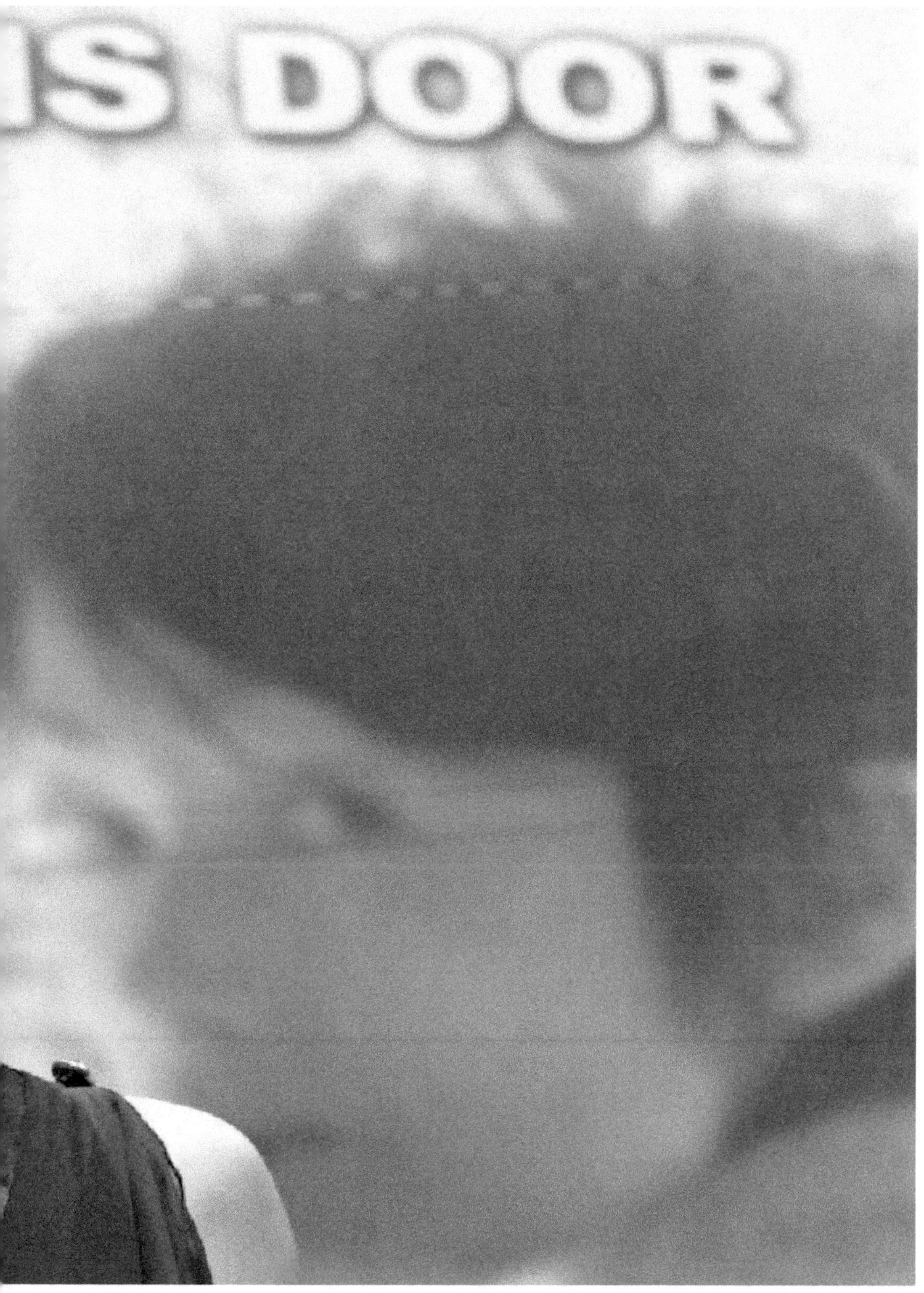
S DOOR

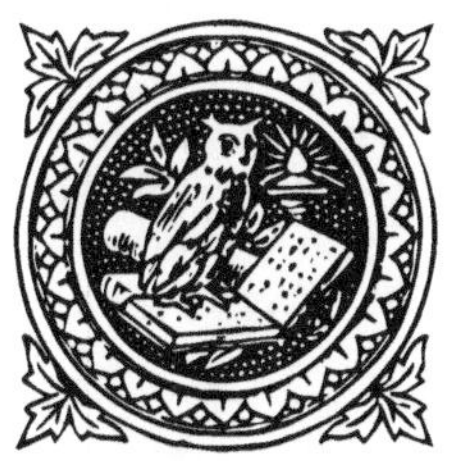

COLOPHON

PLAYS WITH FILMS was typeset in InDesign 5.0.
"Live stage actions" are set in *Legacy Serif Book* 13/16 pt.
"Legends" are set in *Eurostile*.
"Screens" are set in *Legacy Sans Medium*.
"Time signatures" and "Voiceovers" are set in *Consolas*.
"Sound and Music cues" are set in *Legacy Sans Book Italic*.

Book, information design & typesetting: Alessandro Segalini
Cover design: Alessandro Segalini

PLAYS WITH FILMS
is published by Contra Mundum Press
and printed by Lightning Source, which has received Chain of Custody certification from: The Forest Stewardship Council, The Programme for the Endorsement of Forest Certification, and The Sustainable Forestry Initiative.

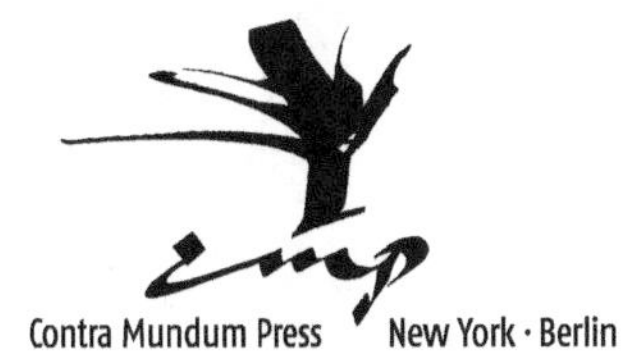

CONTRA MUNDUM PRESS

Contra Mundum Press is dedicated to the value & the indispensable importance of the individual voice.

Contra Mundum Press will be publishing titles from all the fields in which the genius of the age traditionally produces the most challenging and innovative work: poetry, novels, theatre, philosophy — including philosophy of science & of mathematics — criticism, and essays. Upcoming volumes include Miklós Szentkuthy's *Towards the One & Only Metaphor*, Louis Auguste Blanqui's *Eternity by the Stars*, William Wordsworth's *The Sublime & The Beautiful*, and the *Selected Poems of Emilio Villa*.

For the complete list of forthcoming publications, please visit our website. To be added to our mailing list, send your name and email address to: info@contramundum.net

Contra Mundum Press
P.O. Box 1326
New York, NY 10276
USA
http://contramundum.net

OTHER CONTRA MUNDUM PRESS TITLES

Gilgamesh
Ghérasim Luca, *Self-Shadowing Prey*
Rainer J. Hanshe, *The Abdication*
Walter Jackson Bate, *Negative Capability*
Miklós Szentkuthy, *Marginalia on Casanova*
Fernando Pessoa, *Philosophical Essays*
Elio Petri, *Writings on Cinema & Life*
Friedrich Nietzsche, *Greek Music Drama*

SOME FORTHCOMING TITLES

Miklós Szentkuthy, *Towards the One & Only Metaphor*
William Wordsworth, *The Sublime & the Beautiful*
Louis Auguste Blanqui, *Eternity by the Stars*
Emilio Villa, *The Selected Poems of Emilio Villa*
Robert Kelly, A *Voice Full of Cities: Collected Essays*
Jean-Jacques Rousseau, *Narcissus*
Carmine Fahrdor, *The Unbecoming Foreskin of a Dada Mystic*

www.ingramcontent.com/pod-product-compliance
Lightning Source LLC
LaVergne TN
LVHW061219100826
845148LV00004B/803

* 9 7 8 0 9 8 3 6 9 7 2 8 2 *